"Applause is approximately .003% of success. In real life, victories aren't measured by shiny awards and admiring followers. Your greatest victory is to live like Chris Ducker...not trying to be better, but focusing on the tiny but significant differences that actually matter."

—Sally Hogshead, *New York Times* bestselling author of *Fascinate*

"Chris Ducker is the real deal and a true entrepreneur who has experienced the highs and lows of running multiple businesses. This book delivers an important message about how to maintain peace and joy on the journey. You'll be so much better prepared for the long haul once you read it!"

—Rory Vaden, *New York Times* bestselling author of *Take the Stairs*

"Pay attention, leaders—this is the book you've been waiting for! Chris Ducker delivers exactly what burned-out executives need: a practical blueprint for sustainable success without sacrificing well-being. His brilliant strategies will transform how you lead, live, and show up for who and what matters most. If you're ready to move from exhausted to energized and from overwhelmed to focused, this book isn't just a good read—it's essential reading that will revolutionize your approach to leadership. Read it, apply it, and then buy a copy for every leader you know!"

—Neen James, author of *Attention Pays*

"*The Long-Haul Leader* isn't just a book—it's a wake-up call. It took me a few decades to figure out that success isn't about grinding harder, but about leading smarter. Chris Ducker gets it, and he's giving you the road map so you can make the shift now. With honesty, hard-won wisdom, and practical strategies, he shows that real leadership isn't about pushing through—it's about building a life and business that lasts. If you want to skip the burnout and go the distance, this is your playbook."

—Michael Port, *New York Times*
bestselling author of *Steal the Show*

"As someone who used to be caught in the trap of constant hustle, I loved reading this wake-up call for leaders running on empty. With wit and hard-earned wisdom, Chris Ducker shows how to trade burnout for balance and exhaustion for endurance, offering a clear road map to lead with intention and energy, and a vision built to last."

—Erin King, author of *You're Kind of a Big Deal*

"Whenever I get to hang out with Chris Ducker I end up taking notes! If you read this book you'll instantly see why. Some books give you quick wins. This one gives you lasting success. *The Long-Haul Leader* is the ultimate guide to building a business that thrives—without costing you your health, your family, or your weekends! Chris hands you the master key for leading with confidence, growing with purpose, and actually enjoying the journey. If you want to win at business and life, read this."

—Jon Acuff, *New York Times* bestselling author of *Soundtracks*

"Chris Ducker doesn't just tell you to work smarter—he shows you exactly how to design your business around what matters most. *The Long-Haul Leader* delivers tactical, actionable steps to build sustainable success without sacrificing your mornings, your health, or your life outside work. If you're ready to stop glorifying the hustle and start creating real impact that lasts, this is your practical road map forward."

—Amy Landino, author of
Good Morning, Good Life

"If you're feeling trapped in the endless grind of hustle culture, you need this book. Ducker shares hard-won wisdom from his own burnout journey to help you build sustainable success without sacrificing what matters most. An absolute must-read for anyone who wants to thrive in business for the long haul, not just survive the next quarter."

—Pat Flynn, *Wall Street Journal* bestselling
author of *Will It Fly*

"If you're stuck in hustle mode, *The Long-Haul Leader* is the guide you need. Chris Ducker understands what it's like to feel exhausted, work nonstop, and struggle to make time for yourself. But he also shows us a better way. This book is a must-read for entrepreneurs and career leaders who are ready to trade the grind for a more sustainable, fulfilling path to success."

—Jadah Sellner, author of *She Builds*

"Most entrepreneurs start their journey full of excitement, only to burn out because they're doing too much, too fast. *The Long-Haul Leader* is the antidote. Chris Ducker shows you how to build a business that not only grows but also supports your well-being along the way. If you want to succeed without sacrificing your sanity, this book is a must-read."

—Ali Abdaal, *Sunday Times* bestselling author of *Feel-Good Productivity*

"In a world that glorifies hustle, *The Long-Haul Leader* offers a refreshing and necessary blueprint for achieving lasting success without sacrificing what matters most. Chris Ducker knows how to play the long game, and every leader should learn from his wisdom."

—Dorie Clark, *Wall Street Journal* bestselling author of *The Long Game*

"Most entrepreneurs start with passion, but only a few build businesses that thrive over the long term. In *The Long-Haul Leader*, Chris Ducker lays out a powerful framework for creating a business that attracts opportunities, scales sustainably, and positions you as the go-to leader in your space. If you want to build a business that works for you—not the other way around—this book is a must-read."

—Daniel Priestley, author of *Oversubscribed*

"Chris Ducker gets it. *The Long-Haul Leader* is the guide every entrepreneur needs to build a profitable business that doesn't drain them dry. If you're tired of chasing short-term wins and want more clarity on what you should really be focusing on, this book will show you how to play the long game—and win."

—Mike Michalowicz, author of *Profit First*

"All great leaders figure out that the long game is the only game. Why? Because nothing good happens overnight. What we haven't had, until now, is a road map to use to create a lasting impact. I'm grateful Chris Ducker has created this road map for us. If you want to build something that lasts, this is your book."

—Donald Miller, CEO, StoryBrand.ai

THE LONG-HAUL LEADER

Also by Chris Ducker

Virtual Freedom

Rise of the Youpreneur

THE LONG-HAUL LEADER

Ten Strategies to Work Smarter, Live Better,
and Achieve Lasting Success

CHRIS DUCKER

BASIC
VENTURE

New York

Basic Venture
Hachette Book Group
1290 Avenue of the Americas, New York, NY 10104
www.basic-venture.com

Printed in the United States of America

First Edition: September 2025

Published by Basic Venture, an imprint of Hachette Book Group, Inc. The Basic
Venture name and logo is a registered trademark of the Hachette Book Group.

The Hachette Speakers Bureau provides a wide range of authors for
speaking events. To find out more, go to hachettespeakersbureau.com or
email HachetteSpeakers@hbgusa.com.

Basic Venture books may be purchased in bulk for business, educational,
or promotional use. For more information, please contact your local
bookseller or the Hachette Book Group Special Markets Department
at special.markets@hbgusa.com.

The publisher is not responsible for websites (or their content) that are not
owned by the publisher.

Print book interior design by Bart Dawson.

Library of Congress Cataloging-in-Publication Data

Names: Ducker, Chris author
Title: The long-haul leader : ten strategies to work smarter, live better,
    and achieve lasting success / Chris C. Ducker.
Description: First edition. | New York : Basic Venture, [2025] | Includes
    bibliographical references and index.
Identifiers: LCCN 2025000858 (print) | LCCN 2025000859 (ebook) | ISBN
    9781541704831 hardcover | ISBN 9781541704855 ebook
Subjects: LCSH: Leadership | Work-life balance | Success
Classification: LCC HD57.7 .D835 2025 (print) | LCC HD57.7 (ebook) |
    DDC 658.4/092—dc23/eng/20250328
LC record available at https://lccn.loc.gov/2025000858
LC ebook record available at https://lccn.loc.gov/2025000859

ISBNs: 9781541704831 (hardcover), 9781541704855 (ebook)

LSC-C

Printing 1, 2025

To Ercille:
Thank you for being my rock.
Through all our struggles and celebrations,
there's nobody else I'd rather be doing life with.
I love you.

CONTENTS

THE
LONG-HAUL
LEADER

Foreword

I first met Chris Ducker in the way most people do these days—online. I'd been following his work for years, watching as he built multiple successful businesses while maintaining what appeared to be an enviable work-life balance. But appearances can be deceiving.

What I didn't know then was that Chris was about to hit a wall. Despite his outward success, he was running himself into the ground, caught in the same trap that ensnares so many high-achieving leaders: the belief that working harder is always the answer.

I know this trap well because I've been there myself.

For years, I bought into the hustle culture that dominates much of the business world. As the CEO of a large book publishing company, I pushed myself to meet every deadline, exceed every expectation, and be available at all hours. The cost? My health, my relationships, and nearly my sanity.

That's why this book resonates with me so deeply. Chris isn't just sharing theories or recycling tired business advice. He's offering a radically different approach to leadership—one that prioritizes sustainability over short-term gains, wisdom over hustle, and legacy over quick wins.

The *Long-Haul Leader* arrives at a crucial moment. We're living in an era of unprecedented burnout, where leaders at all levels are questioning whether success has to come at such a high personal cost. Chris's answer is a resounding no, and he shows us exactly why—and more importantly, how.

What sets this book apart is its practical wisdom. Chris introduces his LifeOS framework, a holistic approach to leadership that addresses four crucial domains: personal mastery, relationships, hobbies, and impactful work. It's a blueprint for sustainable success that acknowledges a fundamental truth: you can't lead others effectively if you're running on empty yourself.

But don't mistake this for just another self-help book about work-life balance. Chris goes deeper, challenging us to rethink our entire approach to leadership. He shows how the very traits that often drive our initial success—relentless drive, perfectionism, and an always-on mentality—can become our biggest liabilities if we don't learn to channel them properly.

Through compelling stories and practical strategies, Chris reveals how to:

- Set the right pace for sustained success
- Build meaningful relationships that fuel your growth
- Create systems that allow you to work smarter, not harder

- Develop habits that energize rather than deplete you
- Leave a legacy that extends beyond your immediate impact

What I appreciate most about Chris's approach is his honesty. He doesn't sugarcoat the challenges of leadership or pretend there are easy answers. Instead, he shares his own struggles and setbacks, including the pivotal moment when he realized his approach to business was unsustainable.

This vulnerability makes the book's message more powerful. Chris isn't writing from a position of theoretical expertise but from hard-won experience. He's been in the trenches, made the mistakes, and found a better way forward. Now he's sharing that path with others.

The principles in this book have already transformed countless leaders' lives—I've seen it firsthand in my own work with executives and entrepreneurs. But what excites me most is the ripple effect these ideas can have. When leaders learn to work and live sustainably, it affects their teams, their families, and their communities.

If you're tired of the hustle-or-die mentality that pervades much of today's business culture, this book offers a refreshing alternative. It's a guide to building success that lasts—not just in your business but in every area of your life.

Whether you're a seasoned executive, an emerging leader, or an entrepreneur building your first business, *The Long-Haul Leader* provides the framework you need to create lasting impact without burning out in the process.

The question isn't whether you want to be successful—I assume you do, or you wouldn't be reading this book. The real question is: How do you want to get there? Will you sprint until you collapse, or will you learn to pace yourself for the long haul?

Chris shows us there's a better way. And in doing so, he's given us more than just another business book: he's provided a road map for sustainable success that could transform your life and leadership.

I urge you to read this book carefully, implement its principles thoughtfully, and prepare to transform the way you think about leadership. Your future self will thank you.

Michael Hyatt

Founder and chairman, Full Focus

New York Times bestselling author

Hustle Is a Season, Not a Lifestyle

In 2008, after our son Charlie was born, I was pushing hard as the CEO of a call center I owned in the Philippines, working sixteen-hour days, nonstop. Every morning, I woke up with a sense of looming dread and went to bed late, feeling exhausted. I didn't know it then, but the warning signs of burnout were flashing loud and clear, and I was ignoring them.

To make matters worse, our company was in trouble. In a desperate attempt to save the ship, I sent everyone home one day and spent the next two weeks alone in the office, doing some good old-fashioned cold calling. The hope was that by forgoing sleep or any kind of self-care, I could win enough business to keep us afloat another month or two.

It worked—at least, for a while.

For the greater part of that year, though, my life became a living hell. I had to fight tooth and nail just to make it another day. It took everything I had to keep things going. I rarely saw my family and had zero time for myself.

During that time, I switched from employing on-site team members to hiring virtual assistants, which helped cut costs and streamline our overhead, a pivotal move I wrote about in my first book, *Virtual Freedom*. That step transformed my work and opened all kinds of doors for me, but at the time it was just an act of survival. I was doing everything I could simply to keep things going, hustling harder than ever.

In the end, the hustle paid off. The rewards, however, came at a cost (they always do). The company bounced back and continued to thrive, but I had unintentionally formed a bad habit that would eventually catch up with me: *when in doubt, work harder*. Over time, though, defaulting to hustle in a pinch became more and more difficult to do—especially as I got older. Since then, I've learned that you can't always muscle through the latest obstacle. Sometimes it's not enough to work harder. You have to get smarter.

All of us want to show up as our best self in the areas of life where it matters most: at work, with the people we love, and in our personal life. When these areas are firing on all cylinders, most of us feel motivated and energized. We feel successful and full of energy. And as we thrive, we get even more energized to tackle the next challenge. But when these areas fall out of balance, that can have a domino effect, leading to one area of life crashing into another, throwing everything out of kilter.

I didn't fully learn that lesson the first time I experienced burnout back in 2008. But a decade after that first crisis at the phone center, I did. And what I did next changed everything.

BACK TO BURNOUT

Every year, my family and I take a sabbatical. It's become a habit for us, a way to unplug from the world and refocus on what matters most. My wife, Erz, and I spend this time reconnecting with our kids and each other while setting new priorities for the coming year.

In August 2021, we spent the four weeks of our sabbatical in the English countryside. At this point, we were back in the United Kingdom after years of living in Asia. I had gone all in on one of our businesses, Youpreneur, where we serve entrepreneurs building lifestyle businesses around their particular expertise.

After the previous year and a half of transforming this and another company for the virtual world, as a result of all the challenges many faced during COVID, I was tired. Exhausted, in fact. I needed that break.

I approached the sabbatical ready to unload. Nature walks, swimming, and nightly bonfires were the norm. We all had a blast, even the kids, especially our youngest two—Charlie and Cassie—who were my biggest partners in crime when it came to outdoor adventures. We played board games, went teddy bear hunting in the woods, explored the outdoors, and even caught a few Pokémon on our phones.

One night we stayed up late, looking at the stars through a telescope, and as I gazed at my children looking with awe at the night sky, tears welled up in my eyes. I didn't let them see, of course, because that's not "cool." But it was the perfect moment. By the end of the trip, I was beginning to feel the same weariness that had led me to my break in the first place. I couldn't seem to shake it. It didn't make sense. Who *doesn't* come back from a monthlong retreat feeling refreshed and restored?

Like a good soldier, I shook it off and headed back to work. It was typical reentry blues, I thought, that feeling you get when you have to go back to work after a long trip. It would pass. On September 1, I walked back into my home office, turned on the computer, and sat there for ten minutes, staring—unmoving, frozen.

For some reason, I felt just as depleted as I had before leaving on holiday. Worse yet, the usual enthusiasm and passion I typically have for my work was nowhere to be found. I *dreaded* my routine of emails, calls, and projects.

The career I had loved and poured so many years of my life into now felt empty. I felt like I was pushing a rock up a hill only to see it roll back down as soon as I let go. There were goals I wanted to achieve but felt unmotivated to tackle—things I knew I should be doing but had no clarity as to why. Everything was foggy.

I turned off the computer and stepped away, and I didn't turn it back on for another twenty-three days. I just couldn't do it, couldn't go back to work. Not like that.

HUSTLE IS A SEASON

No one can hustle forever. Not Elon Musk, not Gary Vaynerchuk, no one. That's the realization I made that fateful day when trying to return to work. I just wasn't ready. I had absolutely exhausted myself and didn't understand why or how, and it was time to get some answers.

The official diagnosis from my functional medicine doctor was "chronic adrenal fatigue." After getting extensive blood work done, I saw that a lot of my levels were *way* out of whack. No wonder I was so tired. I had been going too hard for too long, and it had all caught up with me. My body had had enough.

The same lifestyle that had gotten me through so many scrapes over the years was now holding me back—way back. The real culprit for my condition was not adrenal fatigue. That was just a symptom of a deeper problem, one that had worked its way into every part of my life. The real enemy was hustle.

Recently I asked some of the business leaders I mentor what they think of when they hear the word "hustle," and they shared the following:

- Working harder, beyond your normal nine-to-five pace
- Experiencing a lack of focus and scrambling in all directions
- Spending less time with friends and family
- Sacrificing what you love most for what you need to do right now

I can relate to a lot of these, for sure, and I imagine you can too. But not all impressions of hustle are necessarily negative. Others talked about how the word made them think of "perseverance," "grit," and "firing on all cylinders." They talked about having the courage to dream big dreams and the tenacity to chase them.

Among the leaders I surveyed, 39 percent saw hustle as positive, 41 percent viewed it as negative, and the other 20 percent had a neutral opinion. In other words, hustle can be a bit of a double-edged sword.

I think of it as the intense pursuit of a single goal, one that requires a lot of energy. At its best, hustle helps us accomplish big things. And at its worst, it can rob us of what we love most. It can be a powerful tool, especially in the life of a leader, but hustle is like rocket fuel: incredibly powerful in short bursts—but also extremely dangerous.

When we don't put hustle in its place, it can wreak havoc on our lives. It needs to be a strategy, not a business plan. You can't hustle forever, and if you think you can, you're in for a rude awakening. Hustle is a season, not a lifestyle.

When I tried to go back to work in 2021, I didn't have it in me. I knew something was off, and I had a decision to make. At that moment at my desk, staring at the computer screen, I realized I could put on the blinders and push through, or I could figure out what was really going on. Thankfully, I chose the latter.

To shut things down and walk away was a privilege and not one I take lightly. Most people don't have any other option than to keep going. No pauses, no breaks, no breathers—just more work. That's why it's so important to recognize the early warning signs of burnout before things really go off the rails, for us all to develop better patterns of work that help us avoid getting to this point in the first place. Which is why this book exists.

In the modern workplace, most of us tend to drive ourselves hard without getting much, if any, relief. But intense, prolonged work has a serious impact on anyone. Continually pushing our boundaries year after year can cause the lines in our lives to blur. Over time, we may struggle to see the difference between our priorities and our obligations.

Granted, sometimes we *do* need to hustle. Going the extra mile or doing one last sprint can be a viable strategy—sometimes. Most leaders have a vision others can't see and a willingness to work harder than most to accomplish that vision. That's leadership.

When you start a new business, for example, you will find yourself in hustle mode, whether you like it or not. You have to put in the extra hours to get this new idea off the ground. And if you don't, no one else will.

But this approach has to be used occasionally. As with a runner calling on reserves of energy to sprint that last leg of a race, hustle is best deployed at key moments and for short periods. When we adopt it as a habit, it's like attempting to sprint a marathon. It just won't work. You might pass your competition at first, but going that hard for too long will eventually hurt.

Hustle is not meant to be permanent. It's meant to serve a purpose. Think of the power and precision of a rowing team— every member throwing all they have behind every push and pull. They're *hustling*, all right, but they're doing it for a reason: to win. Once the race is over, the team takes a break, celebrates their win, and recovers so that they can tackle the next race rested and ready. Then, they start training again.

You're not irrational or a workaholic for working hard. That's good! Wanting to create a better life for yourself and the people you're responsible for is the best reason to push past resistance and go after big goals. Hustle will always take you *somewhere*. The question is whether you are headed where you want to go.

HOW I BECAME A LONG-HAUL LEADER

When I realized my season of hustle had ended and I needed a new approach, I went to work on *myself*. I knew I needed to be more intentional about the choices I was making, and I wanted to give more of myself to the people who deserved it.

I had been depriving myself of physical and psychological nourishment for so long that my life felt empty.

First, I tackled diet, exercise, and mental health. If you aren't giving your body what it needs, everything goes south pretty quickly. To fix the chronic fatigue that had taken hold in my life, I changed the way I exercised, returned to a daily meditation practice, and started eating better. I also got more sleep.

Almost immediately, I started feeling better.

Then I reconnected with old friends and loved ones. I built more moments of connection back into my life. Many of my friends were living in the United States while I was in the United Kingdom, but we made it a priority to reconnect every month on Zoom for happy hours across different time zones. This too invigorated me.

After that, I built back into my schedule regular dates with my wife and scheduled more time with my two youngest children, who were still living at home. It all started to add up to a fuller, more meaningful life.

Finally, I changed the way I worked. Unknowingly, I had slipped back into "hustle mode," working from a place of scarcity instead of abundance. I saw that when I pursued *more* just for the sake of more, I ended up with less of what I really wanted. More work meant less time to enjoy what I'd worked so hard to get. Chasing bigger goals meant less time to celebrate my latest win. I needed more than a break—I needed to get realigned.

Constantly adding more to a never-ending to-do list is a symptom of what Michael Easter calls the "scarcity brain." "Today," he writes, "it's well accepted that for most of human history, obeying the next scarcity cue and constantly craving and consuming more kept us alive. We evolved in harsh environments that had one thing in common: they were worlds of less, of scarcity."

We are all like squirrels looking for that last acorn to tuck away before winter. There's no harm in having more acorns, of course, except when your fear of not having enough leads to a state of constant anxiety. What begins as an attempt to calm our fears actually creates more fear.

Hustle can do the same, getting you over big hurdles but also addicting you to the thrill of having one more problem to solve. Over time, it gets unbearably stressful.

When it came to my own experience, I knew that if I wanted to be around for a long time, I was going to have to start acting like I *would* be. I was going to have to commit to becoming what I now think of as a "long-haul leader."

This meant changing everything from how I worked, to how I lived, to the hobbies I adopted. It meant giving all I could over the course of my life, but not just for the sake of a single goal—for the sake of the legacy I wanted to leave.

A long-haul leader is the opposite of a hustler. They have a long-term vision of the life they want to create and are committed to the process of creating it. They know who they are and what they're about. Long-haul leaders live in alignment with their values on a daily basis, inspiring and empowering others to do the same.

Making the shift from hustle to long-haul leadership was challenging at first but ultimately rewarding. It didn't mean I was no longer interested in winning. It just meant I didn't have to triple and quadruple my goals every year to feel like a success. Mostly, it meant thinking long term, considering the big picture in everything.

My challenge to you, as you read this, is to consider where in your life, right now, you aren't looking at the long-term impact of your actions. Is what you're doing going to get you where you want to go?

In his book *Great by Choice*, Jim Collins documents the success of some of the best-performing companies in the world. He discovered in his research that the highest achievers didn't always crush the competition. Instead they set their sights on achieving better-than-average results over a longer period than most.

The companies that won were the ones that didn't hustle. They also didn't lag behind. They cast a clear vision, set the right pace, and worked diligently to achieve their goals.

Success in life and in business is not about how fast you start but about how far you can go. For some of us, this may be a challenge. It's exciting, after all, to produce a lot of results in a short time, to enjoy the attention success brings. But we only stay in this game long enough to really enjoy it by learning to sustain our success. And that's easier said than done.

Life sends us signs, of course—moments of overwhelm and burnout, gut feelings we just can't shake—but it's up to us to get the message. When life told me the way I had been living was no longer working, I hesitated at first. I was in denial.

After all, I was a healthy guy, took long vacations with my family, and had hobbies. But the truth was I had just gone too hard for too long, and it was going to take a massive overhaul to make the difference.

Eventually, I got the message. I listened to what my life was telling me. It was time to slow down, to find the right pace so that I could go the distance. As a result, my life and work were completely transformed for good.

By doing less of what didn't matter and more of what did, I found a better way of living and working that continues to this day. I'm left now with a clear vision for my life, along with a system that helps me maintain that vision so I will never end up feeling burnt out, empty, or depleted again.

And I want to share that with you.

A PATH TO A BRIGHTER FUTURE

In this book, I'm going to teach you the keys to long-haul leadership—a style of managing your life and work that sets you and others up for long-term success. These are the same keys I've learned in the last couple decades and spent the past several years refining.

What *is* long-haul leadership? It's another way of living, leading, and doing business—one we desperately need now—where we only sprint when necessary. These principles and strategies can help anyone avoid getting stuck in hustle mode or recover from burnout. Better yet, if you follow them early enough, they can help you avoid burnout altogether.

The people who are able to achieve sustained success in their personal and professional lives think differently. They act differently too. The people I look up to, those who have gone the distance in life and business, know how to sustain themselves. They live by the principles in this book.

Each of these long-haul leaders, many of whose stories I will tell in the pages that follow, has a clear and effective system for keeping their head above water and their eye on the ball. But what makes these leaders so different? I've identified ten practices of every long-haul leader, and for the rest of this book, I am going to share them with you.

Here is the overview of where we're headed:

1. **Long-haul leaders set the right pace.** They know going too slow or too fast is a liability.
2. **Long-haul leaders build their lives with intention.** They know the value of a meaningful yes and spend their yesses wisely, knowing they have only so many.
3. **Long-haul leaders invest in meaningful relationships.** They show up for the people who matter most and refuse to take those relationships for granted.

4. **Long-haul leaders make the most of the time they have.** They schedule what's important and set boundaries to protect that time. They also know how to rest in order to return to work refreshed.

5. **Long-haul leaders protect their energy.** They listen to what their body is telling them and make changes to preserve their health and well-being.

6. **Long-haul leaders only hustle when it's necessary.** They recognize that there are times when you've got to push, and they know when and how to do so.

7. **Long-haul leaders focus on the right priorities and let go of the rest.** They concentrate on doing the work only they can do, staying in their Zone of Genius, and automate or delegate the rest.

8. **Long-haul leaders make their money work for them.** They don't let a scarcity mindset dictate their decisions. They diversify their investments, create passive income streams, buy according to an item's value rather than its cost, and build scalable business models.

9. **Long-haul leaders make time for hobbies and activities outside work.** They allow themselves the freedom to pursue activities that enrich their lives, build memories, and bring joy to their lives.

10. **Long-haul leaders leave a lasting impact.** They know they can only do so much in a lifetime and are committed to investing in the next generation.

I want to be one of those leaders. To my friends and to peers. To my colleagues and coworkers. And certainly to my children, wife, and—hopefully someday—grandchildren (you heard me, kids!). I am all in on being a long-haul leader.

For too long, we've been sold the lie of hustle: that to succeed you've got to burn the candle at both ends. In this book, I'm going to introduce you to a different way of living, working, and leading, one that has worked wonders for me and countless others. And if you pay attention, it can work for you too.

This book is my attempt to share the system I learned way too late in life. It's a challenge to live differently. But mostly, it's permission to trust yourself. Life is not a sprint; it's a marathon. And how and when you hustle determines how successful you'll be.

For me, there's no question. I'm in it for the long haul. Are *you*?

CHAPTER 1

In It for the Long Haul

Long-haul leaders set the right pace.

E very runner knows that the pace you set determines when and how you finish a race. Go too fast, and you risk getting injured. Run too slow, and you'll lose. But when you find your stride, you feel like you could run forever. There's nothing like that feeling of flow, when it's easier to keep going than it is to stop.

The same principle applies to business—and life. When things are just working, you can feel that momentum. It's just *easy*. Unfortunately, that feeling can be elusive. It's impossible to bottle, let alone sustain. Most leaders are so blinded by their passion that they don't think much about pacing. They're too excited to realize that they may be going too fast or pushing their team too hard for that momentum to last long.

Many of us tend to do this at some point, for one reason or another. Maybe we feel like we can't slow down. Or we're just so used to going hard for so long that we don't even realize how unsustainable our pace is. Whatever the reason, if we keep going, it won't work.

The way you win a race is the same way you finish well in life: you have to set the right pace. Sadly, it's often not until we find ourselves on burnout's doorstep that we realize something has gone terribly wrong.

HITTING THE WALL

When we keep working harder and harder to pursue bigger and bigger goals, while continuing to put the most important areas of life on hold, we may eventually find ourselves hitting what runners call "the wall."

The wall comes in almost any long race. It's the inevitable moment when how hard you've been working and how long you've been going finally catch up with you.

And then it hits. You don't think you can move another inch. You lose your energy, your will to go on; everything hurts. There's no hope for taking another step.

But any experienced runner knows this is not the end— it's an opportunity. To recalibrate. To adopt a new strategy. To find a way to keep going.

This is true in life. Hitting the wall—burning out—is a chance to reinvent who you are and what you do. It's a dare to get serious about what really matters. This isn't a sign to stop. It's an invitation to realign, reassess, and get the right resources so you can finish well.

You may not have hit your wall yet. You might still be working hard, pursuing a big goal, thinking you're indestructible. But trust me when I tell you, if you're going hard without taking time for yourself and the rest of life, your wall is coming. And at that point, everything that was once easy will be difficult. For many of us, it's not a question of *if* but *when*.

When this happens, it's not time to throw in the towel. It's time to dig in. Not to push harder but to step back. Burning out is a chance to reinvent who you are, to get clear on what you want your life to be about. To do this well, you have to know what your priorities are and give them the attention they deserve.

For many of us, this includes work. But if we only cut back on work without building up our relationships, health, and hobbies, we're still not going to have enough gas in the tank to make it very far. We have to think more holistically.

Becoming a long-haul leader begins with getting clear on your priorities, making a commitment to honor what matters most, and creating a plan to reinforce these priorities. Long-haul leaders pay attention to what matters most without neglecting what needs to be done now—they set the right pace.

SETTING THE RIGHT PACE

It's no surprise to my friends and family that I'm a competitive guy. I don't like to lose. And I certainly don't know how to try only a little. I'm either all in, or I'm well and truly out. Most entrepreneurs I meet are the same. No one gets into the game of business aiming for mediocrity. They want to win. We all do. We want to create something that lasts, something that inspires others to do their best, something that brings out the greatest contribution in all of us.

We want to be the best in the world at what we do, whatever that is. And to be the best, you can't play small. You have to zoom out, see the whole field, and figure out what it's going to take. Sometimes this means stepping back and saying no to short-term obligations so that we can plan more for the long term. This is what I told my nutritionist and functional medicine doctor, Nicole Goode. Although I had started working with her on what *I* needed, she soon became a client of mine after she started feeling like she had maxed out her current business opportunities and was stuck in a no-scale scenario.

The traditional business model for doctors, especially within her specialty, is to see patients one-on-one, as she did with me. It's what all her peers do and what most people expect of her. But because of this model, Nicole's schedule was filled to the brim, and she was turning away clients she really wanted to help. She felt guilty, exhausted, and frustrated.

At the same time, this situation was hurting Nicole's cash flow, because many of her patients didn't want to work on their health during the holidays. They wanted to stay up late eating sweets and drinking eggnog. So November and December were always dead months, revenue-wise, and that left her feeling anxious and restless about money at the end of the year.

I asked Nicole if she was willing to do some things differently, to break the mold of her industry and rethink her business model. Most importantly, though, I wanted to know if she was open to helping more people. She said she was game, so we dug in.

I encouraged Nicole, instead of continuing to meet with clients one-on-one, to think bigger. What could she do if she could do anything? Together, we designed a group-coaching program where she could provide education to more than a single client at a time and help people improve their health across several key areas.

For Nicole, this was the best of both worlds: her clients would get exclusive access to her, but she could also share her expertise at a level that helped her reach more people and make more money. Within a few days of launching this new program, she landed ten new clients and received a massive influx of cash.

She started offering this program throughout the year, which allowed her to make more money, especially during those lean months at the end of the year. She also was able to serve more people *and* spend more time doing what she loves.

Before we started working together, Nicole told me that her instinct was to just keep pushing harder, to just keep doing more of what she was already doing. That's hustle mentality, and after a while, it just doesn't work. Eventually you can't keep giving more. You've got to think bigger picture than simply applying more effort to the same old problems.

Nicole started to feel this, as she'd been growing tired of the daily, weekly, and monthly grind of trying to get more clients. It was beginning to burn her out. What she really needed was a new perspective. And once she stepped back and focused on a more strategic approach to her work, she felt invigorated by her business. Today she's making a bigger impact than she ever anticipated or hoped, and she's never been happier.

Nicole still works one-on-one with clients, but these are now her highest-paying clients, not those she needs to pay the bills. They are the kind of people who are willing to invest more in themselves, and as a result Nicole enjoys working with them.

With all the extra time she gained from her scaled programs, Nicole wrote a book, which is another way to bring more people to her work. This was an audience she never would have reached before. And she's just getting started.

When you shift from a shorter view of life to a longer-term vision, you get long-term results. Focus on the right priorities at the right time, and the right outcomes will come.

THE WORK-LIFE BALANCE MYTH

It has been said you can go fast or you can go far—but you have to choose one. When people start to feel the pangs of hustle culture, they tend to believe that they need to find a better "work-life balance." As if "work" and "life" are two sides of a scale that we can tip this way or that, adding a little more here or a little less there, and it'll all even out. But that's not how life works.

The truth is work-life balance isn't real. There's no way to keep those two areas completely separate from each other. In these days of constant communication and remote work environments, "life" tends to collide with "work" in more ways than one. It's impossible for one not to eventually bump into the other on occasion.

Many of us were raised with the expectation that work is separate from the rest of life, especially family. We grew up believing that you could check out of your job at the end of the day. And if you brought it home with you, that was the exception, not the rule.

But now that's all changed.

You might be working, deeply focused on a task, and suddenly you get a call from the doctor's office and have to drop everything. Or you're trying to relax with family, and you see your boss has copied you on yet another email that requires immediate attention. Whatever headspace you were in has now immediately shifted.

More than ever, work is invading our daily lives, and life is constantly interrupting work. It's just the situation most of us are in most of the time. When we ignore this reality, we set ourselves up for disappointment and frustration.

The antidote to this problem is not to ignore work or to put off all our personal goals and ambitions for later. We don't need to balance work and life so much as we need to integrate the two.

How do we do this?

We begin by giving enough of ourselves to the right thing at the right time. We go fast enough to finish the race but not so fast that we're going to injure ourselves or hurt others, including our family, in the process. This is what setting the right pace means.

Only you know the right pace for you. Work is not the enemy, but it can become a problem when it's the most important area of life and you aren't balancing it with the other areas that depend on it. Your family, friends, and hobbies are not getting in the way of business. Your personal life can fuel your work and vice versa. You need both, and to integrate them well, you need a plan.

DON'T JUST PLAN TO LIVE—LIVE THE PLAN

As the CEO of a large publishing company, my friend Michael Hyatt was chronically busy for years. At the neglect of his personal health, Michael worked himself to the bone, pushing to meet every deadline and exceed the expectations of his board members and team. This went on for the greater part of a decade.

It was difficult, but Michael told himself it wouldn't be forever. Sadly, he was right. Such a grueling pace is unsustainable for anyone, and it eventually catches up with you, which it did with him.

Being a strong type A (like myself!), Michael had created a "life plan" for himself that included specific goals regarding taking care of his health. In that plan, he had strategized every aspect of his life and work, including time he wanted to spend on hobbies and making key memories with family members. There was just one problem: he hadn't gotten around to doing most of what was in the plan.

One year, on a work trip to New York City, Michael started having chest pains over dinner with a friend. Convinced he was having a heart attack, he rushed to the hospital only to be told nothing was wrong. He went home feeling confused.

This happened two more times in the next year until a cardiologist told Michael that these were panic attacks caused by years of stress. My friend heard the message loud and clear and got serious. It was time to live the plan.

In the following years, Michael got his health in order. He didn't just make a plan—he took action on it. He started eating right, exercising regularly, and giving his body lots of rest.

Michael monitored his stress levels and spent time doing the things that brought him joy. He raised up new leaders in his company and handed a lot of the day-to-day management of the company over to others so that he could focus on creating the kind of impact he wanted his life to have.

At first Michael was afraid his work might suffer as a result of his refocusing on other areas of life that weren't solely work. He worried the company he was leading might lose money, that he would be seen as a failure.

But the opposite happened.

With his priorities in the right place, Michael's work flourished, as did his well-being and relationships. He got healthier, reconnected with his daughters, and even took up fly-fishing. Everything in his life got better, richer, and more meaningful. He reinvested in his marriage and started playing the guitar again (something he hadn't seriously done since college).

This is what happens when we shift from a life of constant hustle to one of long-haul leadership. It's not always easy, especially in the short term, but the more you focus on setting the right pace, the more you are able to accomplish.

Obviously, it's easier to make plans than to execute them. But planning can only get you so far before it's time to take action. A key mistake most people make when attempting to right-size their priorities and get their lives back in order is to focus way too much on the plan. Planning to live is fun, but if you never live the plan, then you're missing the point.

I used to spend all year hustling, overworking for the reward of my annual sabbatical. When I did this, I was pinning my hopes on a future date when I would eventually get to enjoy time with family and do what I wanted. Is it any wonder I burnt out more than once? Even a sabbatical couldn't fix that.

But slowing down and deciding *where* I wanted to go and what was a sustainable pace for me changed everything.

In the next chapter, we'll talk specifically about how to do this. We'll learn how to set the right intentions for how we live and work, and I'll introduce a powerful framework that will help you make better decisions and prioritize what's most important to you.

But for now, I want to ask you a simple question: *Is the pace at which you're living and working right for you?* Forget about what everyone else is doing. You have no idea how happy they are or are not—how close to burning out they may be. At any rate, it doesn't matter. This is your race, after all; it's your life. Do you just want to go fast, or do you want to go far? The pace you set will determine whether or not you can go the distance.

CHAPTER 2

You Get More of What You Focus On

Long-haul leaders build their lives with intention.

In early 2017, my family and I purchased our dream home in the English countryside. But it was far from perfect. As it was a historic estate, we were going to have to do a fair amount of work to bring it back to its full glory.

We planned a 2018 move from the Philippines, where we'd been living for years, back to the United Kingdom, where I had grown up and spent the first part of my adulthood. This timing would allow us the space we needed to turn our three-hundred-plus-year-old property into a family home.

To celebrate the return, I started dreaming about a big party.

At first, I didn't have a lot of direction for the event. Selfishly, I just wanted a reason to get all my friends in the same room and make a big splash. But as we started thinking about it and making plans, I realized we could make it something really special.

The community side of our Youpreneur brand had grown substantially since its launch in 2015, and we now had hundreds of members all over the world who relied on us to help them grow their businesses. My team and I had been running events over in the Philippines a couple of times a year now, including our popular Tropical Think Tank—which we hosted for five years in a row.

We'd also held small Mastermind events in the United Kingdom, United States, and Australia over the years. These were intimate get-togethers for business leaders where we would drill into each entrepreneur's struggles and help them solve the problems they were facing. It was fun and impactful work when we could get people together, but our community was still very much scattered across the globe. This upcoming move was our chance to bring clients from around the world together and forge new relationships, as all these incredible like-minded entrepreneurs could come together to break bread.

I soon saw what this could be. It wouldn't just be a party. With a renewed purpose, we realized that we were on to something special. We were now planning a conference.

We called it the Youpreneur Summit.

With our *why* now solidified, the rest of the project was practically effortless. We quickly prioritized what needed to be done leading up to the event. We picked the right speakers, created a schedule, and focused on crafting an experience our clients would love.

To show just how important our community was to us, we hosted it at the Queen Elizabeth II Convention Center, directly opposite the beautiful, iconic, and historic Westminster Abbey. We had pulled out all the stops.

The event ended up being a smashing success, and I'm glad I didn't stop at "let's just have a party." We went deeper and got in touch with a more meaningful purpose and intention that allowed us to pull off an amazing experience for ourselves and others, one filled with moments and memories many still treasure to this day.

KNOW YOUR WHY

The antidote to aimless hustle is getting grounded in your values. You have to know why you do what you do if you want to stop doing things that don't ultimately matter to you.

We've all heard about the importance of knowing our *why*. Business leaders have been talking about the significance of mission and vision for decades. But, as Simon Sinek said in his now viral TEDx Talk, "Very, very few organizations know *why* they do what they do."

That's true. In his work, Sinek provides an illustration of how our values fuel our actions, something he calls the Golden Circle: a bull's-eye comprised of three concentric circles.

The outer circle is our *what*, the middle circle is our *how*, and the center circle is our *why*. Most companies start with *what*: a product they want to create or a service they want to provide.

Then, they ask *how*: "How will we create and deliver that product or service?"

But seldom do they ever get to *why*.

As a result, many individuals and organizations build their lives and work around what they do and how they do it, but few are clear on why they're doing what they're doing. *How* and *what* are, of course, important questions, but they will only take you so far on any journey. To go all the way, you need to know *why*.

We can tell when someone doesn't have a clear purpose guiding them, and we can tell when they do. When you know why you're doing what you're doing, even the biggest challenge can become manageable. In contrast, when you aren't clear about why you're doing something, the smallest obstacles can start to feel insurmountable.

Simon Sinek's solution is to *start* with why. Don't wait until later to find a reason or a purpose for your work and life. Know your *why* now, then figure out how to design and deliver solutions that align with it.

Most of us tend to start things without thinking through the consequences (like "Let's throw a party!" or "I just want to make more money"), and only after thoughtful reflection can we align with a deeper, more meaningful reason for why we're doing what we're doing. This is okay. But if you want to do something for the long haul, you're going to need a deeper purpose. So why not *start* with it?

THE POWER OF SMALL STARTS

Sometimes your why is not a carefully planned strategy. Sometimes, you just stumble upon it, trying to solve a simple problem. When Sergey Brin and Larry Page began collaborating on the early iterations of what would later become Google, they were graduate students at Stanford, steeped in academic pursuits. They didn't even like each other.

In a culture where everyone was required to consistently publish new papers and cite other people's papers, Brin and Page saw an opportunity. Papers are judged by how many *other* papers cite them, which is something you can easily measure. Soon the two men saw an interesting connection.

As a student, Larry Page imagined the new and emerging technology of the World Wide Web as a graph where webpages were like academic papers and the links back and forth were like citations. If he could find a way to catalog and organize these links to show how the pages connected to each other, then the authors of those pages would understand where they ranked—just like in academia.

The project Brin and Page used to test this model, called "BackRub," organized and ranked the number of backlinks each webpage had. It was a simple start, a solution to a felt need. But that was it—nothing grandiose, no big purpose behind it other than a fun way to connect ideas to each other. Only later, as the Internet grew and the two men realized the full potential of what they had created, did they expand their *why* to something more. Today, Google's stated mission is to "facilitate access to information for the entire world, and in every language."

Nowadays, the tech startup isn't just organizing links so that other academics can figure out where they rank. Google offers dozens of services and products all designed to make information easy to find and organize. This is a purpose that aligns with the needs of billions of people on the planet, which is, indeed, a very big *why*.

Since those early days, Google has expanded beyond search to help people organize their entire digital lives: from email to document storage to business communications and much more. But it didn't begin that way. Few big things do. Don't ever worry about solving too small a problem or having too small a purpose to begin. That's where most things start.

You don't have to have some big purpose for your life or work. Not yet, at least. Knowing why you're doing what you're doing is reason enough to keep at it. The *why*, over time, will expand, but don't feel intimidated if it's modest at first. When in doubt, start with a simple solution to a real problem. And over time, see how it expands. Just like Google did.

FIND THE RIGHT PROBLEM TO SOLVE

Most of us tend to see a problem and look for the fastest way to solve it. We think we want a *what*, not a *why*. Then our scarcity brain takes over, driving us into a frantic state of hustle that only ends up causing more harm than good.

This was where Nick, a past client of mine, was when he jumped on board one of my mentoring programs. He had lost a handful of recurring clients in his coaching program because one disgruntled customer had decided to start his own business, taking several of Nick's clients with him. Nick needed to bring in new clients quickly, so he lowered his prices. He filled up spots easily enough. But his other existing clients caught wind of the discounted rates and complained. He had to pass on the lower price to them, cutting into his own anticipated profit margin.

Nick had made the mistake of "robbing Peter to pay Paul," a decision that would end up haunting him for a good while. Not until our team helped him reflect on the purpose for his coaching and refocus on *why* he wanted to serve his clients did he land on a new and improved version of his business that felt even more valuable.

You see, Nick was a life and business coach who worked specifically with fathers who had experienced loss in their lives: divorce, business failure, health issues, or any other distressing event. Nick had gone through a tough divorce himself and knew how hard it was to be a good dad through life's ups and downs. He was passionate about helping other men like himself overcome the unique challenges they were facing.

Once he had refocused on this purpose, he started attracting new clients. Before, he had been holding biweekly in-person sessions with clients and giving them unlimited email access to him. After our work together, Nick started holding monthly calls, with in-person visits limited to a quarterly basis.

He also stopped communicating with clients via email and started using Slack instead for more timely responses. Not only did his clients get more in-person time with him where he was able to provide a higher level of care and attention, but his time on email was cut down, and he was able to respond to clients' needs more quickly and efficiently.

It was a win-win scenario. And it all started with Nick's getting clear on why he was in business in the first place. If you haven't taken the time to figure out the reason you do what you do, it's not too late to figure it out. Knowing your why makes everything clearer.

Don't worry about trying to justify the decisions you've made in the past. That's done. We only need to focus on what's ahead. Knowing why you're making a decision helps clarify the purpose behind it and attaches values and beliefs to your goals and aspirations, making everything you do matter more.

Don't let your past dictate your future. Let your *why* be the guide.

THE LONG-HAUL LEADER LIFE OS™

For businesses like Google, having a mission statement that encapsulates one central, driving force for products and services may be sufficient. But life doesn't always work that way.

Most of us don't just have one *why*. We care about a lot of different things, and to come up with a mission statement that only covers one aspect of who we are and what we care about often feels inauthentic.

After speaking with friends, mentors, and peers, I started to paint a clearer picture of an operating system that could help me, and others, focus on the interlocking pieces of life. I landed on four basic areas that any person can use to define the direction of their life—I call it your life operating system, or LifeOS. Here's what it's made up of:

+ **Personal mastery:** Becoming the best version of yourself, including your physical health and personal expertise
+ **Hobbies:** Doing different activities for relaxation, enjoyment, and just plain fun
+ **Love and relationships:** Spending time with family and friends in meaningful ways
+ **Impactful work:** Doing things as part of both your job and your life's accomplishments that ultimately feel meaningful and important

Without any one of these elements, something would be missing in my life. Yes, I love my family and my friends, and I also find meaning in my work. Work is fun, and I also take a handful of hobbies seriously. I enjoy eating well and taking care of my body, and I also find satisfaction in relaxing. And, of course, I want to push myself hard to accomplish big goals and master new skills, and I want to enjoy the process of getting there.

Life gets better as we realize each of these four areas depend on one another. These domains intersect and overlap, creating a Venn diagram we can use as a filter for making better decisions.

You'll see on the image several overlapping sections. These represent how different areas of life influence each other. The elements in the overlaps (time, memories, freedom, clients) are

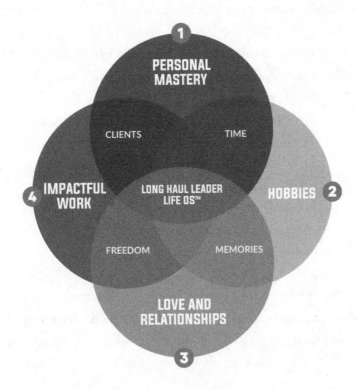

crucial because they highlight what you gain when two focus areas work in harmony.

Personal Mastery

+ **Time:** This represents how mastering yourself gives you control over your time. The better you become at self-discipline, productivity, and personal growth, the more time you unlock for things that truly matter. It's about using self-mastery to create space for what enriches your life.
+ **Clients:** Mastering your personal skills and abilities makes you more valuable to your clients. It's the intersection of expertise and service to others—helping you serve at a higher level, attract the right clients, and thrive in your work.

Hobbies

+ **Time:** Hobbies demand time, but they also offer the chance to relax, recharge, and gain new perspectives. When you dedicate time to hobbies, you're investing in personal joy and creativity, which indirectly benefits your overall effectiveness and well-being.
+ **Memories:** The intersection between hobbies and relationships creates memories. It's about the lasting experiences and shared joy that come from doing things you love, either alone or with others.

These moments enrich your relationships and personal satisfaction.

Love and Relationships

+ **Memories:** Relationships are where memories are made. The more you invest in hobbies and personal time with loved ones, the more meaningful moments you create. This intersection highlights how both quality time and shared activities build strong, lasting relationships.

+ **Freedom:** When love and relationships intersect with work, freedom comes into play. Strong relationships give you the support and stability to pursue your passions, and meaningful work can, in turn, provide the freedom to spend time with the people you love.

Impactful Work

+ **Freedom:** Impactful work isn't just about earning money—it's about creating a life that supports your freedom. The work you do should empower you to live on your terms, which, in turn, enhances your ability to nurture relationships and pursue personal passions.

+ **Clients:** When personal mastery aligns with impactful work, you gain clients who resonate with your expertise. This represents the external result of doing meaningful work—attracting people who see the value in what you offer and allowing you to make a bigger difference.

Over the years, I've tested and perfected this framework and discovered that it creates a lens not just for helping myself and others remember what's important but for making decisions. It's an incredibly useful tool and can help you build the habits needed for long-term success.

GETTING INTENTIONAL ABOUT THE FUTURE

Our *why* is about knowing where we're coming from. You can't know where you're going until you have a real sense of where you've been. Otherwise, you end up repeating the past.

The only way to improve is to start with what you've already accomplished, then figure out how to do better next time. Which is why we have to set intentions—to know where we're headed in life.

It's easy to set goals, and I'm sure you have set a number of goals in your life. But as I've gotten older, I've realized the importance of intentions. They are about looking forward and deciding where you want to go and what you ultimately want to do. Intentions are open-ended, filled with possibility and opportunity, but guided by and grounded in a person's purpose.

To set clear intentions, you have to ask yourself three questions for each domain of the LifeOS:

+ What do I really want?
+ What am I willing to give up to get it?
+ What are my nonnegotiables?

Answering these questions will help you define what matters most to you, what you really want, and what you need to focus on to get it. Forget what others call "success." Decide how you want to show up in each area of your life and optimize for that—and only that.

A few years ago, when I realized how hard I had been running for so long, I started setting new intentions for my health. Asking myself these questions helped me figure out what I wanted this area of life to look like and how I would begin to take the steps to fulfill that vision.

Here's how it worked: I asked myself a series of simple questions that helped me get realigned around my intentions.

1. What Do I Really Want?

This is always the question you should ask when you're struggling with meeting a goal that you just can't seem to hit. Sometimes things aren't working because you aren't being honest about what you want or why you want it.

Why wasn't I as healthy as I wanted to be? It was really a question of motivation. I thought I needed to be healthy but didn't have time for it. When I saw the cost of this behavior, though, I started getting serious—and honest—with myself. I needed more energy so that I could show up more fully at work and at home. What I was doing just wasn't working: my kids could see it, my wife could see it, and now I could see it. Enough was enough. It was time to make some changes.

2. What Am I Willing to Give Up?

Nothing comes for free. Everything has a cost. When it came to my health, I knew that what I had been doing, on some level, was easier than what I knew I needed to be doing. But the pain of staying the same was now greater than the pain of change. At this point, I was willing to sacrifice quite a bit, because I knew the risks of not making such changes. I knew the cost of continuing to eat poorly and not exercising, as well as not getting to bed on time.

It was all beginning to catch up with me, and I was ready to let go of my old, bad habits to adopt some newer, better ones. I saw clearly that what I wanted was worth what I needed to give up to get it. That's how you know the change is worth the cost.

3. What Are My Nonnegotiables?

Changing your life isn't easy, and you probably won't be able to do it all at once. It's a marathon, remember? So consider what is essential for you, what's absolutely necessary. Some days, you'll be able to do only these essentials; other days, you might be able to do more. Knowing what matters most, what you simply cannot live without, will help guide you. These are your nonnegotiables.

First for me was sleep. I had to get more, much more, which I did by setting a goal of being in bed by 10:30 every night. I have to go to bed and wake up at the same time every day—it's just, I've learned, how I'm wired. Without consistent rest, I'm miserable and exhausted most of the day. So there's no fudging on this one.

To help with getting to bed early, I use blue-light-blocking glasses for ninety minutes before turning in, which helps me downshift at the end of the day and get ready to fall asleep. It works wonders.

At first enforcing an earlier daily bedtime for myself wasn't easy. I wanted to stay up! I had shows to catch up on with my wife, emails to answer, and work I could still do. But I knew the cost of those old habits and was no longer willing to negotiate on what I knew was best for me.

By simply forcing myself into bed earlier, even when I wasn't tired, I started organizing my day around that bedtime. And before I knew it, my wife and I were in bed by 10:00 or 10:30 and asleep within thirty minutes. Sometimes you just have to put yourself in the right place to make good habits easier.

Next on my list of nonnegotiables was exercise. To start this habit, I began doing moderate exercise on a regular basis, prioritizing getting to the gym at least four days a week. Now it's the first thing I do most mornings. On the days that I don't work out (usually two to three days per week), I rest and recover from the previous day's workout. On those mornings,

I read a book with a cup of coffee or spend some time with my wife before getting to work.

Other nonnegotiables include my monthly chiropractic adjustment, a monthly deep-tissue massage, and clean eating. When these habits began, I definitely still had a bit of a sweet tooth, but I pretty much went cold turkey with sugar. I don't particularly enjoy eating fish, but now I eat it three or four times a week, because I know I need the nutrients.

I also threw daily red-light therapy into the mix. And although the full-body panel I purchased cost a pretty penny, its benefits—such as muscle recovery, reduced inflammation, and increased energy—made it a no-brainer. I also have a full medical checkup done annually, as a promise to myself to stay on top of my health.

As I've integrated all these new habits into my routine, I've found that they have become essential to maintaining my energy and being able to show up as my best, healthiest self every single day. You can't get far in life if you don't prioritize your own well-being and make room for the changes that need to happen.

Now It's Your Turn

Making a big change is as simple as asking those three questions about what you want, what you're willing to give up to get it, and what your nonnegotiables are. Take a minute to ask yourself these questions in each of the four domains of the LifeOS framework—and see how aligned you are with your values.

As an example, let's take the "Love and Relationships" domain.

First, ask yourself, "What do I really want when it comes to my relationships?"

Maybe it's more time with a spouse or just less time working. Maybe you have aging parents you want to visit more often or simply more free time. (Remember: it's hard to hit a moving target, so try to get clear on what your intention is for this area of your life.)

Then, ask, "What am I willing to give up to get it?"

Everything has a cost. The more we prioritize something, acknowledging what getting it takes, the more likely we are to accomplish what we set out to do.

And, finally, consider what you are not willing to give up to get what you want.

Knowing your boundaries will ensure that you don't burn yourself out in pursuit of your latest goal. The nice thing about this is that you tend to know when you've lost sight of an intention. Sometimes the clues are obvious. If I don't get good sleep or miss my chiropractic adjustment, I am uncomfortable, irritable, and hard to deal with. Everybody can tell, including me.

But sometimes I know more through intuition. My gut rarely lets me down, and I know it's time to reconnect with my *why* when I start losing enthusiasm for what I'm doing. I'll bet you know what your warning signs are as well when you start to feel stuck or misaligned.

HOW TO BALANCE COMPETING PRIORITIES

Everyone hits roadblocks and challenges at one point or another in life. A project at work stalls, we stop making the progress we wanted to see on our personal health goals, or maybe we start feeling really tired.

These are signs of misalignment.

But what do you do then? Do you see the roadblock as a temporary setback, as something to power through? Or do you find yourself struggling to get out of bed in the morning? Dreading what's in front of you is a sign that you're pursuing the wrong thing. Don't delay making major changes now. If you don't, you may regret it later.

But sometimes, the signs are subtler than that. The other way to know your intentions aren't clear is that the different pieces of life start to compete with each other. If you find yourself feeling resentful of the way a work project is cutting into your time with family, this is a sign you need to set better intentions for work and how you show up for your family.

To do this, you may decide to designate one evening per week to catch up on work, leaving the rest of your time free for family or hobbies. Or you might decide, "My new working hours are from 8 a.m. to 5 p.m. on weekdays, no exceptions."

The point is that your intentions should shift as the four domains of your life evolve. Don't feel like you have to commit to these things forever. They are meant to be useful ways of managing what's important to you, so feel free to come back to them as often as necessary to reassess what's working.

By keeping intentions malleable, we don't have to cut one of our core domains completely out of our lives. Many of my clients discover that impactful work, relationships, and personal mastery are all they can handle—and often in that order, if they're being honest.

But when I ask about hobbies or what they do for fun, they look at me like I'm crazy. *Who has time for that?*

Most of us put dreams and hobbies on the back burner in pursuit of more pressing matters, like family and work. That's only natural. But if we're not careful, years can go by without our ever moving the needle on some of our biggest aspirations. If enough time goes by, we might lose our excitement for life altogether.

Don't give up on your dreams; they're important. But you have to be careful with how you pursue your dreams while balancing the rest of life.

What if instead of thinking, "I want to write a book in the next six months," you said, "I want to write 500 words every single day first thing in the morning"? Or instead of saying, "I want to become a chess master," you began with "I want to learn ten new chess strategies this year"?

Suddenly, the hobby you might have been tempted to quit becomes more doable, even easy. That's the power of setting intentions that fit with the rest of your life, seeing how all the domains work together to create a life you love.

Being intentional helps us add more enjoyment back into our lives, even while we continue to have busy work and family lives. These habits keep us happy and healthy, so long as we don't lose sight of what's important.

DON'T LET THE URGENT DISTRACT FROM THE IMPORTANT

The pandemic was devastating for thousands of businesses, shuttering restaurants, gyms, retail stores, and other establishments that depended on foot traffic. But business had never been better for a small sector of the US economy: technology.

This was certainly the case for Zoom, a once little-known video conferencing software. As CEO Eric Yuan wrote in a blog post in April 2020, "Usage of Zoom has ballooned overnight," boasting 200 million users doing approximately 10 million daily meetings.

In a panic, Zoom rushed to hire 800 new staff in 2020 to help manage the increased usage—a nearly 50 percent increase. And in the next two years, it nearly quadrupled its staff. Zoom, it seemed, would never fall.

And yet, when we experience unexpected growth in business, it often becomes the new expectation. During the pandemic, growth became the new norm for many booming tech businesses, and shareholders demanded CEOs find ways to maintain the same level of growth even when the world reopened, inflation hit, and business returned to prepandemic levels.

It didn't work.

While Zoom's employment skyrocketed, its growth fell by about 50 percent by 2023, and it was forced to face the music, laying off many of the people it had just hired in the previous three years.

In another blog post, Eric Yuan wrote, "We worked tirelessly and made Zoom better for our customers and users. But we also made mistakes. We didn't take as much time as we should have to thoroughly analyze our teams or assess if we were growing sustainably, toward the highest priorities."

Most of us probably would have done the same thing. Yuan was responding in a predictable way to the urgency of the situation and likely hoping for continued growth, but the company had lost sight of its *why*: "one platform delivering limitless human connection."

The assumption is that Zoom wanted to do that indefinitely, but the company fell into the trap of pursuing indiscriminate growth, without planning for that growth. Many leaders do the same, prioritizing the urgent to the detriment of the important.

How often, for example, do we react to someone's mistake, responding in the heat of the moment, rather than taking time to respond calmly and productively? How often do you work late in response to a client's or boss's demand to have something ready as soon as possible, instead of respecting your own boundaries?

We all have a tendency to give in to short-term pressures at the expense of long-term health and happiness. The only way to avoid falling into this trap is to maintain a relentless focus on your LifeOS and the intentions you set for each domain—and to protect them at all costs. Imagine that Zoom had pursued a more balanced approach to expansion, hiring a bit more prudently and slowly to see if the bubble would burst.

By 2022, many workers had returned to their physical offices, and workplaces no longer needed a video conferencing tool to run smoothly. Zoom also might have explored partnerships with other service providers to help take some of the pressure off their business. Scaling the workforce more gradually would've meant avoiding at least some of the drastic layoffs in 2023. For most of us, when we start saying yes to the things we shouldn't, we run into trouble.

EVERY YES IS A NO

Your intentions mean nothing if you don't protect them with what you say yes—and no—to. Let me explain.

Many moons ago, I received an invitation to speak at a blogging event in Las Vegas. It was my dream opportunity—my chance to break out and make a big name for myself in the US online business industry.

I had attended the event before, and something about being on that stage was important to me. In fact, I had been wanting to speak there for some time, but I was unsure of what the application process looked like and couldn't seem to find a way in.

And then, this invitation dropped into my lap.

Because I didn't have much of a speaking career under my belt, however, the event organizers weren't going to pay me. Nor were they going to pay for my flight or hotel. Everything would be up to me, with the benefit of "exposure." It's a common deal many aspiring speakers and thought leaders make. And like others, I said yes because I really wanted to speak at the event.

Thankfully, we had clients in the United States at the time, so I could put the cost down as a legitimate business expense and tag on visits with a couple of our clients in California, which was relatively close to Las Vegas, considering my company was based in the Philippines. Still, it was a massive expense and a major risk. What if nothing came of it?

About two or three weeks later, I got an email request from somebody who had been following me for quite some time on social media and was an avid listener to my podcast. He wanted to hire me for a full day's in-person consultancy on how to build a remote team around his accounting business.

He offered to pay my daily consulting rate and for all of my travel. The only problem was that he wanted it the same day as the blogging conference, and he was based in Australia. Unfortunately, he couldn't move the date.

I ended up saying yes to the conference and no to the paid work but later regretted it. If I'm being honest, I accepted the free speaking gig because of my ego. I didn't receive anything from the opportunity. And by saying yes to the event, I said no to building a stronger relationship with an already devoted client and making a lot of money.

It really is true that every yes is also a no.

THERE'S ALWAYS A COST

My son Charlie and I love building LEGO sets together. It's one of our favorite things to do.

A few years ago, we decided to build the Star Wars Death Star, which has over 4,000 pieces altogether. It's complicated and intricate (and expensive!), and it requires intense concentration to complete. When we got the set, Charlie was ecstatic. We had been talking about building it for months, and now it was finally happening.

At the same time, however, my company was in the middle of a launch for our Youpreneur Incubator. I tried to stay present with the LEGO build, but while I was there with Charlie at the table, my phone kept going off like mad. I was getting constant Slack notifications from my team for one thing or another relating to the launch.

I would build a bit and then have to be back on my phone for a couple of minutes, then build something before taking a quick call or sending a message. It wasn't an enjoyable experience for either of us.

Every time I said yes to a notification popping up on my phone, I was saying no to being present with my son. I could have stayed present and built another core memory.

But I allowed the short-term urgency of the outside world to intrude on one of my most important intentions: to be fully present with my kids.

This happened years ago, and I learned my lesson (not to make conflicting commitments to both family and work). And yet, here I am still talking about it. When you lose sight of your intentions, you end up agreeing to do things you later regret, and those regrets can haunt you for years. Be careful what you say yes to, because at the end of the day, your yeses are an asset. And if you start signing up for too many things, they quickly become a liability.

STOP, STAY, START

We should say yes to our areas of greatest value and contribution, which means developing the discipline of saying no.

To help you stay focused on the right intentions, I'm going to teach you one of the most helpful tools I use with my clients and with myself. I call it "Stop/Stay/Start." The Stop/Stay/Start exercise, as the name suggests, helps leaders decide which areas, initiatives, or products in their businesses need to be stopped, which ones need to stay (and perhaps shift), and which new projects should be started.

In today's business world, many entrepreneurs feel guilty for taking time to enjoy their lives. However, the sooner we can embrace the discipline of saying no, the faster we can start making better decisions for ourselves and our lives.

The exercise is simple. Here's how it works. Ask yourself the following questions:

+ "What's not working that I should immediately *stop* doing?"
+ "What needs to *stay*? What should I keep doing that is essential to the kind of life I want to live and work I want to do?"
+ "What's missing in my life and work? What do I need to *start*? If I had more time, what would I feel excited about working on?"

This is a process of regular reflection, and getting it right takes some time and practice. But once you start doing this, you will be unable to continue doing things that don't make much sense for very long.

Recently, I used Stop/Stay/Start with one of my Mastermind members, Jenni Field. At the time, Jenni and I were in Portugal at my Round Table Mastermind retreat for coaching clients. It was a beautiful place, right in the middle of paradise, but she was stressed.

Jenni had a lot on her plate at work and was in a bit of a funk about it. One of the goals she really wanted to accomplish was writing a book—and yet, I knew she had more pressing issues to deal with in her business. As her mentor, it was my job to walk her through what changes and decisions she needed to make in the last quarter of the year.

Together, we discussed all the important tasks she had on her list. She was in danger of missing her sales goals if some of these responsibilities didn't get met. She had client proposals to send, meetings to hold, and end-of-year analyses to get done. The one thing she did not want to do was delay her plans for the book.

But that's exactly what I told her to do. For now, I told her, writing the book was something she needed to *stop*.

At this point, the book was a nice-to-have, not a must-have. It was an important personal goal for her, but it wasn't critical to her business, and prioritizing it over her company would have serious detrimental effects.

After dinner one evening, we were walking back to our hotel, talking it all over. Jenni realized she could write her book later—if she did it right then, she might not have the business she needed to make the book successful. Saying yes to something always means saying no to something else. And vice versa.

We also talked about what in Jenni's business needed to *stay*. In her situation, it was the highly personalized client work her customers needed and valued. That was something only she could do, and no one else could do it for her.

And as for *start*, the answer, at that time, was nothing. That's okay too. You don't always have to be starting new things, especially when you've put so much on the back burner that needs your attention now.

Jenni made the decision to push the book back and doubled down on what she was doing in her business. She cleaned up a lot of back-office issues that had arisen in the previous months. She tended to some of the challenges that had come up with her staff and followed up on proposals and leads to get as much business through the door as possible.

It worked. Jenni smashed her quarterly sales goal, ending the year on a high note, and in January, after just a few months of delaying work on the book, she restarted her writing project, this time with a solid foundation. Last I spoke with her, she was in the final editing stages of working on the manuscript.

When we're overwhelmed, it's easy to lose focus, to forget what really matters and stop making the right choices. We end up worse off than we would have otherwise been. But the more you build intention into each area of your life, the more quickly you'll start reaping the rewards. Now, let's see how this works within our most precious relationships, which is the subject of the next chapter.

CHAPTER 3

"Who" Is What
Really Matters

Long-haul leaders invest in
meaningful relationships.

One of my favorite memories includes running from a nest of angry hornets. Let me explain. It was 2014, and I was speaking at the Tribe Conference in Nashville, hosted by my friend Jeff Goins. I had been online friends with another speaker, Dan Miller—author of *48 Days to the Work You Love*—for years and was excited to meet him in person.

Dan lived nearby and graciously invited Erz and me to breakfast at his house the morning after the conference. At breakfast, Dan's wife, Joanne, served biscuits—which, to me, looked like English afternoon scones. I thought serving biscuits for breakfast was brilliant!

Throughout the meal, Dan and his wife made us feel welcomed in a way we didn't expect. He listened patiently and asked thoughtful questions, genuinely interested in getting to know me and supporting my work, even though I was decades younger than he.

I was also impressed with the way he and his wife so obviously adored each other and the way he spoke about their children. I immediately felt Dan could be a valuable friend and mentor, not only in business but in life and family as well.

After our breakfast, we walked around his property. Dan had an old rusty car sitting in a lovely spot, surrounded by trees. I stood by the hood to take a picture with it and, without thinking, banged my hand on the hood appreciatively.

Suddenly a swarm of angry hornets rushed out from under the hood to attack me. Dan stood at a distance, chuckling and taking pictures as I ran away with the speed and agility of a teenager, screaming. Thankfully, I wasn't stung. On many occasions over the years we laughed about that memorable start to our friendship.

Erz and I went away from Dan's house that day with a handful of books and life lessons. I knew, viscerally, that we had connected and were going to have a close friendship over the course of many years. Dan felt it too.

And we did just that.

Although we lived on different continents (and both ended up moving away from where we started our relationship), we messaged each other often and caught up every few months via Zoom.

Every year, Dan and I made it a point to see each other in person—usually at a conference where we were both speaking. No matter how busy we were, we made time to break bread to continue cultivating our friendship. It became a nonnegotiable. Over the years we'd send each other our books, celebrate one another's successes, and continue to invest in our relationship. We both knew early on that this was a friendship worth cultivating.

Dan passed away in January 2024.

I spent most of that month reflecting on what he had meant to me as a friend and mentor. Above and beyond anything else, his legacy reminded me that I could chase *more* in my life—more money, better health, more passion—but nothing would enrich my life more abundantly than meaningful relationships.

AN EPIDEMIC OF LONELINESS

In 2023, the US surgeon general released a headline-making report titled "Our Epidemic of Loneliness and Isolation."

The eighty-two-page report shed light on an alarming problem: people are not just suffering in isolation; they are suffering *because* of isolation.

Under President Barack Obama, this same surgeon general, Vivek Murthy, had embarked on a listening tour of the United States, hoping to learn more about what worried people most about their health. He was shocked to find that the top concern wasn't cancer, heart disease, diabetes, or Alzheimer's.

It was loneliness.

In doing further research, he learned that loneliness is in fact a major health concern. In his report, he writes, "Loneliness is far more than just a bad feeling—it harms both individual and societal health. It is associated with a greater risk of cardiovascular disease, dementia, stroke, depression, anxiety, and premature death. The mortality impact of being socially disconnected is similar to that caused by smoking up to fifteen cigarettes a day, and even greater than that associated with obesity and physical inactivity."

As a leader, you probably know that loneliness is a problem, especially for executives and managers. In 2012, a survey of CEOs showed that about half of them felt lonely in their positions. But this isn't just an issue for those at the top. Workers at all levels experience profound loneliness.

The stakes are higher than ever, especially following the COVID-19 pandemic, which confined most of us to our homes and accelerated the trend toward digital communication instead of authentic, face-to-face communication and connection. Most of my clients were forced to downsize their businesses, scale back, and completely reimagine their roles as entrepreneurs and business owners. And they had to do it mostly alone.

I was in the same boat. And as I am an extrovert, the isolation drove me crazy. Beyond crippling health, loneliness is one of the biggest obstacles to long-haul leadership. I've seen over and over again that lonely leaders make bad decisions, indulge in unhealthy coping behaviors, and consistently compromise their values.

When leaders operate in isolation, they miss out on the perspectives and insights of others. They lack someone to hold them accountable. They don't have a sounding board to test ideas or help them stay focused on what matters most. Worst of all, loneliness deprives us of hope.

WHY WE NEED DEEP RELATIONSHIPS

Relationships are foundational to life. They make everything more enjoyable and meaningful. Don't take my word for it, though. Just ask psychologist Abraham Maslow.

In 1943, Maslow created a framework for understanding what motivates people, known as the Hierarchy of Needs. You've probably heard of it.

Using this framework, Maslow argued that all humans have five basic categories of needs, and these impact almost all of our actions and behaviors. These five categories are arranged in order from our most basic to our highest needs. At the bottom are physiological needs, such as food, water, shelter, and the like. The next levels are safety and belonging, where relationships come into play.

But relationships play a role as we move higher up Maslow's hierarchy as well. The highest levels are self-esteem and self-actualization. These levels are about feeling fulfilled and purposeful, like our life matters. Often we define fulfillment and purpose *through* our most meaningful relationships.

If you're a parent, you know exactly what I mean by this. Life tends to take on a deeper meaning when kids come along. The relationships we have with our children become central to our identities. This connection—not just with kids but with others—is how we know we matter.

When I surveyed my own audience, over 60 percent of leaders and entrepreneurs said that building strong relationships was a major growth area for them. They knew they needed deeper connection with friends, partners, and colleagues but struggled to build that connection.

Deep relationships are among the most vital pieces of long-haul leadership. They help us stay focused on what matters and hold us accountable for living out our intentions. Whether we realize it or not, we are all hard-wired to seek out and sustain close relationships. It's the only way we really grow and stay healthy.

Long-haul leaders don't leave relationships to chance. They know how to invest in them and continue cultivating relationships with others. They make the effort to connect, going as deep as they can in a relationship. Hornets and all.

THE HALLMARKS OF CONNECTION

Think about your closest relationships. What makes them different from your other, more casual friendships? I can think of a few things. Five things, in fact, which I call the "hallmarks of connection."

1. Shared History

Shared history is built by doing life together and making time to be present with the other person. This isn't easy, and you can't rush it. In turn, these are the people we turn to when tragedy strikes and problems arise, when people get married or divorced and welcome new additions to their families.

Having the support of a person who knows you, who's seen you through good and bad, will always make challenging experiences more bearable. We all need friends like that.

This is how it is with my friend Kaveh.

Kaveh and I met when we were both thirteen and became friends because of our shared love of basketball. We played on the same school team, on the same borough team in tournaments, and even on the same national team at Crystal Palace in London. Kaveh and I spent so much time together and in each other's homes that he knows my life story better than anyone else.

One of the things I treasure most about our friendship is that we can reminisce about my mum cooking him meals and joking around with my dad at dinner. Because of our shared history, I can relive some of the happiest moments in my life, revisiting my parents who are no longer around anymore. It's a true gift.

Not only that, but Kaveh and I continue to build new memories together. I have pictures of him holding each of my four children when they were babies, who all know him affectionately as "Uncle Kav." That's a special relationship, and I don't take it for granted.

2. Mutual Respect

In a meaningful relationship, you don't have to always like the other person, but you always have to respect them—and vice versa. Mutual respect ensures you seek equality and fairness in the relationship more often than not.

All relationships will be a little unbalanced at times. There's a natural give-and-take in any kind of connection between people. Sometimes our circumstances dictate that we need more support. Other times, we will be in a position of offering that support to others. Mutual respect makes it safe for each person to advocate for their needs and set boundaries so that no one feels they're being taken advantage of.

3. Mutual Influence

Relationship researcher John Gottman has found that the willingness to accept a partner's influence is one of the foundational elements of marriages that work. Accepting influence is not about caving to pressure or being a doormat, though. It's about staying open to and flexible about someone else's opinions and suggestions. It's about taking what they say seriously and integrating their thoughts and ideas into your decision-making.

Of course, this isn't only essential for marriages. It's crucial for all kinds of partnerships and friendships. And it's harder than it looks.

How many times, after all, have you made a suggestion to your spouse only to have them roll their eyes and say, "Sure, whatever you want"? Have you ever felt obligated to ask for a peer's input but already prepared an argument for why you feel your idea is better?

Most of us are ready to defend our thoughts and emotions long before we've listened to someone else. We don't realize that approaching these conversations as negotiations prevents us from building a true and deep sense of connection.

4. Vulnerability

Relationships are a risk. They mean opening ourselves to hurt and disappointment. In her bestseller *Rising Strong*, Brené Brown writes, "Vulnerability is not winning or losing; it's having the courage to show up and be seen when we have no control over the outcome."

That's the hardest part. Letting go of control. I'll admit I'm not very good at it. But I've gotten better over the years, and my relationships have prospered because of it. As I've learned to be more vulnerable with my friends, wife, and children, I've been surprised to find that it almost always opens the door for deeper connection—the kind of connection you get only by taking risks. Sometimes this means admitting your failures, asking for help when your pride doesn't want it, or just going first.

5. *Honesty*

Sure, you can be in a relationship with someone you're not honest with. But you won't experience the benefits of a real relationship with that person. And if they're not a person you feel safe being honest with, that's probably a relationship worth reevaluating.

Nothing works without honesty.

Obviously, this is easy to talk (and write) about and way harder to put into practice. Connecting requires more of us than disconnecting. As with most good things, it asks us to take the harder but ultimately more rewarding path. So how do we get there? How do we build purposeful relationships that last? We do what we do with anything we value. We invest more in what we want more of.

RELATIONSHIPS REQUIRE INVESTMENT

I often tell clients that the path to better relationships is investment. Deeper connection with others is not something that happens "naturally." It takes intentionality. After all, our relationships should be treasured.

On that note, let me tell you about one of my best mates, Pat Flynn.

Pat and I came up at the same time online—both blogging, podcasting, and creating videos. We ran in similar circles and often spoke at the same events.

In 2010, he and I officially met in person for the first time and had an immediate bond because of our shared connection to the Philippines. Pat is half Filipino. His mother is from Cebu City, where my wife is from, and where I lived for nearly eighteen years. On top of that, his wife, April, is also Filipina, and our wives became fast friends.

At first our relationship was about business. We learned how to become better speakers, practicing in our hotel rooms at midnight before presenting the next morning, giving each other feedback, and acting as audience members for one another—always cheering each other on and helping one another grow.

But as we've both become dads and watched our online careers evolve over the last decade and a half, our friendship has shifted into something deeper. Like Dan Miller and I, Pat and I have made a point to see each other as much as possible, despite the many miles between us.

When I visit San Diego, I always stay with Pat. Once he came all the way to the Philippines just to visit me when I lived there. More recently his whole family stayed at our home in the Cambridgeshire countryside.

Now we both want to focus on the important things, like being good partners to our wives and creating memories with our families. We all prioritize making memories together, calling each other our "second family." I know this friendship will last until the day I die. Why? Because we keep investing in it.

Imagine each of your relationships as its own bank account. You make positive deposits over time to build up equity with each other. These deposits can be as small as a "thinking of you" text or as big as flying across the ocean. The point is that it takes effort to create connection. There are no shortcuts.

For one of my Round Table Mastermind members, a small relationship investment made all the difference and has led to long-term flourishing for her and her family.

When Joana Galvao was twenty-two, she attended one of my one-day Mastermind events. There were ten people in a room for a whole day, all sharing questions and struggles about business and entrepreneurship.

At the time, Joana didn't like her job, didn't like having a boss, and saw way more potential in freelancing. Living in London at the time, she was limited in how much she could go back to Portugal to visit her family. Working for herself, she hoped, would provide that opportunity.

At the event, Joana picked up a handful of strategies for meeting her goals. But it was when we all went out for drinks at a nearby pub that everything clicked for her. While we were all hanging out, just chatting casually, I point-blank asked her, "Why don't you just quit?"

"But my mom," she started to say. "She's not gonna approve."

I tried to prod gently. "Why is that so important?"

We kept going, digging deeper. She eventually started crying, and I kept encouraging her, trying to not push her too hard or let her off the hook too easily.

"You've got this," I told her. "You're gonna quit, and you're going to be really successful."

That one conversation led to an entire career change for her. Soon after, Joana quit her job and started offering freelance design services; she now runs a graphic design agency that serves some of the biggest thought leaders and companies in the world. Best of all, she and I are still good friends, and I continue to support her in all she's doing.

Recently, the two of us caught up, and Joana said to me, "Sometimes, I wonder. What if we hadn't all gone out to the pub that day? What if we didn't have that conversation? I probably wouldn't have wanted to carry on."

Relationships matter. How we connect with others affects the outcome of not only our lives but the lives of others too. We can't take this lightly. As in financial planning, the size of an investment is not what matters most—it's the consistency. Investing a little bit over time is more likely to yield greater results than investing a lot all at once.

The same is true for relationships. If you give a little bit to the right things, over a long enough period, the investment will pay dividends. More from you will beget more for the relationship.

Withdrawals are bound to happen, of course. We all have times when we need support from the people in our lives. And we all know people who need help on occasion. But be sure to keep making deposits when you're able, because otherwise the relationship will decline. Some people may see your lack of commitment as a sign of how you view the relationship and feel like it's one-sided. Safeguard your relationships like you would a pile of cash. They are the most valuable asset we will ever possess. Let's try not to take them for granted.

REMOVE DISTRACTIONS TO CREATE MORE CONNECTION

Often the opportunity for greater connection is right in front of us, but other, less important things get in the way. This is especially true with our spouses, partners, and the people we spend daily life with.

A good friend of mine, Shawn Stevenson, is the author of *Sleep Smarter*. And in that book, he writes, "The bedroom should be for two things primarily ... 1) sleep and 2) we'll get to that in just a moment. ;)"

To keep the purpose of the bedroom focused on those two things, Shawn says some things simply have to go. This includes TV, work, and your phone.

A couple of years ago, I started noticing that my wife and I weren't spending as much quality time together. We had gotten into the habit of scrolling on our phones as we lay in bed together each evening. We would still be talking to each other, but we were not truly *together* in those moments.

We were each doing our own thing in a space that is meant to be for intimacy—not just sex, but true connection. The bedroom should be a place for deep conversations, laughing, and resting. Instead, we were filling it with other, less important things. We both felt the effects, but we allowed the habit to carry on for a bit.

Eventually, I turned to her one night and said, "You know, I don't like the way that this is going. We're getting into bed late at night and we're sleeping later into the day because we're on our phones. We can't turn off our brains. We're not talking in bed as much, we're not cuddling in bed as much as we used to. We need to put some boundaries in place so that we don't get distracted when we're with each other."

Erz agreed.

We then made the rule that we would only charge our phones at bedtime, outside the bedroom. Then we took the television that was in our bedroom and put it downstairs. Making those two simple changes has led us to be a lot more intimate.

My wife and I live busy lives. We've got two older kids to stay in touch with and two younger kids in school. They've got their own social activities, playdates, rehearsals, and other events.

Erz and I also run a business together, so there's not a lot of time to talk about personal stuff during the day. The only time we get to be on our own without interruptions or distractions is in bed. So this was an especially sacred time and place that deserved our investment and protection.

Once we started connecting more in the evening, we found that we wanted to connect more during the daytime as well. We now take "Fri-dates" every week, going to a bookstore, grabbing brunch together, or popping into a yoga class.

What's the lesson? More begets more. More intimacy leads to more quality time, and vice versa, in a cycle that keeps us strong. Ditching the screens has made all the difference in our relationship. I won't tell you to do what we did, but I will encourage you to invest in what matters most and in those you care about. Let your LifeOS guide these priorities, then stick to them, especially when they involve the ones you love the most.

Erz and I started pushing this boundary even further into our family life. Now, when we're out and about, we don't allow the kids on phones or screens if it's family time. So often you go to a restaurant and see parents chatting away while kids play on screens, ignoring each other. Our family doesn't do that anymore. Now, when we're at a restaurant, we're *really* together, talking and having fun. We talk about the food, tell stories, ask questions, and create moments of genuine connection.

I want to be the dad my kids continue to call when they're in their twenties and thirties and beyond. I want them to like me, even after they're old enough to realize all the ways I might have messed up. I want my wife to continue to feel her needs are being met—emotionally, relationally, physically, you name it. I want to make sure we don't take each other's presence for granted. It's too easy to forget that there are no guarantees, that relationships require constant attention and care. These kinds of moments don't come often enough, and I never want to let another one pass me by.

MAKE EXTRAORDINARY
MEMORIES TOGETHER

When my son Charlie was about five, we took him to Disneyland in Anaheim, California. Together, we did everything: went to the studios, walked down Main Street, took pictures with all the Disney characters, and rode every ride he could go on.

At the end of each ride or activity, we had to exit through a gift shop, and Charlie loved it. He shouted, "I want, I want, I want!" More than we should have, we gave in for the sake of a little peace and quiet.

By the end of the day, after waiting in lines, paying for overpriced food, and listening to Charlie's demands, I was exhausted, overstimulated, and honestly a little grumpy. But I remember walking back to our hotel that evening and seeing the smile on his face. He was having such a great time—which made it worth it.

I left feeling like the trip had been a success. We were really making memories and living the dream. Or so I thought.

Five years later, my family and I were at Hong Kong Disneyland. There on Main Street, ten-year-old Charlie met Woody from *Toy Story*. He was over the moon. We took pictures, and Charlie exclaimed, "I can't believe I got to meet Woody from *Toy Story*! This is so cool!"

Puzzled, I said, "You've met him before, mate. You met him in Los Angeles when we went to Disneyland in America. Remember?"

"Wait," he said. "I've been to Disneyland in America?"

It killed me.

He had absolutely no recollection of the experience at all. We'd had a great holiday, but it didn't make any lasting impression on him, not the way we had hoped. And it certainly wasn't worth all the costs and hassles of the day. Note to self: Don't take our younger daughter to Disneyland until she's older!

Looking back on it, I didn't expect my five-year-old son to remember everything we did during that Disney visit. But I did expect him to remember some things. I was hoping there would have been some core memory of our time together that he might treasure, some feeling of family. But he remembered nothing. We've got lots of photos for him to look at, but he doesn't remember a single thing from that day.

And honestly, I should have predicted that.

We had good intentions taking Charlie to Disneyland. Even if, because he was so young, he didn't remember the particulars of that trip, we hoped it would provide an opportunity for bonding as a family.

But if I'm really being honest, there was nothing meaningful about that trip for any of us. Nothing against Disneyland. We were there to be entertained, and we got exactly that. But being stuck in my own head, complaining about the prices and the food, didn't exactly leave a lot of room for connection with my kid.

Reflecting on all this reminded me of another experience.

When my oldest son, CJ, was ten, he loved to paint these little lead figures from a role-playing game called *World of*

Warhammer. The game involves an array of mythical fantasy creatures: orcs, dragons, knights, wizards, that sort of thing. The game has been around for decades, and I used to paint these figures when I was the same age CJ was.

I remember how I loved the process of picking the figures, priming them, painting them, then displaying them proudly for friends and family.

That year, when we were visiting the United Kingdom from our new home in the Philippines, I took CJ out one day for a shopping excursion. After lunch, we went down to the Warhammer store, and I bought him some figures and a whole bunch of paint. There were a couple of new detail brushes that he really wanted, because the brush he had at home was not small enough to paint the faces and other details on the figures.

I got the new brushes for him.

The clerk put all the supplies into a plastic bag, and as we were walking down the street, CJ said, "Thanks, Dad, for getting all this stuff. You're the only one who understands."

I knew what he meant. I remembered being the only kid with that hobby and how alone I had felt. In that moment, we made a sweet connection.

Since then, CJ and I have discussed that moment at least half a dozen times. It's amazing the details he still remembers, like walking out of the store with that plastic bag. My oldest son is a grown man now, and that memory stays with both of us to this day. I believe we'll remember it forever.

These are the kinds of memories we want to cultivate with the people who matter. It's not about doing something extravagant. It's about paying attention to the small details and staying present in life's everyday moments. That's where the magic happens.

STAY CURIOUS ABOUT CHANGE

My friend Bryan and I met at a sports bar in late 2000. He was running his own telecom business with clients in the Philippines, while I was there working for an international bank. It wasn't long before we discovered that we were both lifelong supporters of the Boston Celtics—I, from London, he, born and raised in Boston.

We stayed friends, and although we now live on different continents and Bryan has moved on from being an entrepreneur and returned to working in a corporate setting, we've done our best to remain close. He's visited my company premises and attended my wedding. He is also my youngest son's godfather and has been involved in multiple core memories for our family. But even for close friends, life has a way of pulling you apart.

Bryan and I hadn't seen each other in person since 2017, but the 2024 NBA Finals provided the perfect excuse for us to get together in Boston and cheer on our beloved Celtics in game two against the Mavericks.

The day of the game, we did a tour of the TD Garden, walked around the executive and hospitality suites, posed for photos with statues of Larry Bird, and grabbed a slice of pizza and a beer. We relived some of the fun times we had in the

Philippines together over the years, and then it was time for the game.

At the big game, we high-fived, cheered our Celtics, booed the Mavericks, and hugged and jumped up and down like kids. It was awesome!

The next day, we drove to Bryan's mum's house. She's getting on in years now and doesn't get out that much, but as an avid watercolor painter, I couldn't pass up an opportunity to get a quick lesson from her—she's an incredible artist. Bryan sat and listened in, took photos, and then afterward thanked me for giving her some time to shine. Another core memory!

And of course, Bryan and I jumped on FaceTime when "we" won game five at home, clinching the Celtics' eighteenth championship.

Up until this point, my friend and I hadn't seen each other much in recent years and hadn't done a great job of staying in touch. Our different lifestyles—I'm a family guy, and Bryan is single—and different career focuses, not to mention different time zones, all played a part in hindering us from staying close. But when we found a reason to reconnect, we took it.

Not every relationship has to last, of course, but I think all of us want some to stand the test of time. Remember that having a shared history is one of the hallmarks of true connection and a meaningful life.

What makes most relationships difficult to maintain is that we change. In fact, life is one long obstacle course, filled with all kinds of changes, some planned and some not. Marriage, divorce, children, loss, moves, retirement, financial struggles, medical problems, and more all add to the challenge. And none of us gets out alive!

The only way to maintain close personal and professional connections over time is to remain curious. You have to be curious about the person you are becoming, how you are being shaped by all this inevitable change, and who the other people in your life are becoming. When you embrace change as an opportunity for growth and exploration, relationships become an adventure, one where you continue to meet the people you already know.

In the face of life's inevitable twists and turns, those you are connected to make most things worthwhile. Don't neglect this part of life, as money and success will come and go, but some friendships can last a lifetime. The most valuable way we can invest in other people is with our time. And in the next chapter, I'll show you how to protect that time so you can spend it well with the ones you love.

CHAPTER 4

Master Every Moment

Long-haul leaders make the most
of the time they have.

You can tell a lot about someone's life by looking at their
schedule. What we give our attention to is the most
powerful sign of what we value. So take a look at yours,
right now, and see what it tells you.

Have you, for example, scheduled time for exercise and
eating well? What are you learning right now? Is any of the
free time on your calendar protected? When do you plan to
rest and do something fun?

And how are you prioritizing the important people in
your life? Are you working on the right priorities? Do you

have enough time to accomplish what would actually bring you fulfillment?

If you're like most people, your schedule probably looks a lot like mine once did. Not too long ago, my typical day was a marathon of putting out fires, scouting new opportunities, wining and dining with clients, and traveling (or getting ready to travel). It was all work and no play, and it did indeed make me a very dull person.

Time with Erz and the kids happened in the "cracks" of the day: a quick lunch here, an attempt at a meaningful chat there, a last-minute visit to the gym squeezed in when something else fell through. It was not good. But I was going so hard for so long, I honestly didn't know how to create space in my life for what, and who, mattered most.

When life came crashing down, I got the wake-up call and knew it was time to reevaluate everything. When I did, I didn't like what my calendar told me. The things I said I valued . . . I clearly didn't.

So I set out to change that. You can too.

FIRST THINGS FIRST

One of the greatest pieces of advice I ever received was from my friend Michael Hyatt when he said, "If it doesn't get scheduled, it doesn't get done."

I completely agree and have lived by that quote ever since. Anything important in life should go on the calendar, no matter how big or small. That's how you make time to live your intentions instead of just talking about it. Because, as you know, what's urgent isn't always important.

I used to let time for the important things like my health, my family, and my hobbies get taken over by more seemingly urgent tasks, like budget meetings and calls with unhappy clients. Things that someone else on my team could have easily handled stayed on my task list—and schedule—because I didn't take the time to decide what was truly important to me. As a result, my schedule was overrun with obligations that I didn't get excited about.

Today my life is much different. I remember my nonnegotiables. I keep my priorities. And, taking Michael's advice, I put those things on my calendar first. The work will always be there, of course. But you don't want to take everything else for granted. If you don't prioritize it, it won't get done.

Here are just some of the things that go on my calendar before I start work calls, client meetings, or other commitments.

In addition to the "Fri-dates" Erz and I share, we have our Wednesday evening date nights scheduled indefinitely into the future. I also exercise first thing in the morning. Even though I know I'm going to do it every day, it stays on my schedule, because it's important.

Then every month, I have a ninety-minute full-body deep-tissue massage and a chiropractic adjustment. These appointments are nonnegotiables, and my work life gets scheduled around them.

It's important to schedule white space into your life as well. This is time that you can choose to spend however you wish. I have an hour after lunch (also protected) each day, between one and two o'clock, that is always blank on my schedule.

My wife, my team, and anyone who has access to my calendar knows that this hour is off-limits for work or other appointments. This white space is important because I use it to either play catch up, do deep work, or rest. I can sit and read a book or sketch for half an hour if I want to. It's up to me to use the time how I want—and no one else can ever lay claim to it.

Protecting this space is critical and part of what feels like freedom to me. It's rewarding to know I have the flexibility to get out my sketchbook and do a quick drawing or take a nap if I choose.

In my LifeOS, I try to make sure all four domains (personal mastery, hobbies, love and relationships, and impactful work) are in balance. Of course, there are times when necessary admin tasks need more attention or family requires more of me. But for the most part, I'm mindful that if any single domain starts to take up too much time, the others will suffer.

Everything I do for work—from private messaging with Mastermind clients to calls with team members—goes on the calendar as well. I have weekly calls with my chief operating officer, Chloe, even though we also talk throughout the course of the week on the phone and via Zoom.

The biggest commitment that gets scheduled on my calendar is no work on Fridays. I keep Fridays as open as possible for my "Fri-dates" with my wife or for travel, especially if I'm going on vacation. Friday is completely off-limits and has been for nearly a decade. My team knows this and respects the boundary, which is one of the best perks of being the leader and owning your own business. *You* get to decide the ground rules for your schedule. If something is important, it becomes a nonnegotiable and needs to be scheduled.

If you don't respect your time, others won't either. There's no point in putting it on your calendar if you allow work calls to get scheduled during free time anyway or if you agree to move that blank space "just this once." Do this and don't be surprised when people trample all over your boundaries. Or, on the other end of the spectrum, watch in amazement as people respect your boundaries when you are clear about your priorities.

WHAT'S THE RETURN ON INVESTMENT?

We can spend our time in a million ways. So we have to learn which ones are worth our energy and attention. When my first book, *Virtual Freedom*, came out, I went on as many podcasts as I could to talk about the book. I said yes to every single interview request that came through and reached out to a lot of people as well.

In the one month surrounding the book launch, I had over sixty interviews scheduled. I soon realized, however, that about 70 percent of those interviews were a complete waste of time. Either the show wasn't relevant to the people I'd written the book for, or it wasn't big enough to make an impact. I was casting too wide a net, trying to manufacture momentum, and it didn't work.

I learned that just because we *can* do something doesn't mean we *should*. This is a hard habit to break, especially for us high performers and people pleasers. But finding the right boundaries for what we are willing to say yes to is essential to living the long-haul life.

When I was first learning to drive, I wound through heavily built-up areas with my driving instructor, Vanessa, in the passenger seat. The speed limit was 30 miles per hour, and no matter where I was, I was intent on making sure my speed hovered around that mark: 29, 30, 32, 30, 31. Eventually, though, Vanessa pulled me over and turned the engine off.

"Chris," she said, "we need to talk about how you keep driving up to the speed limit. That's not needed. It is a speed *limit*, not a speed *target*."

This lesson stuck with me, especially in my career. Yes, more could always be done. But if we want others to not expect constant performance from us, if we ever want to take a break, we first have to stop expecting it from ourselves. We don't always have to push ourselves absolutely to the max.

During my book launch, I realized that just because I *could* get on all of those podcasts didn't mean doing so would be worth it. Most of the shows I was on weren't relevant to my topic and didn't reach the right audiences. It was a lot of work for very little reward. I sold way more books off a dozen well-chosen interviews than I did based on all the other ones put together.

Lesson learned: always make sure the work you're doing is worth the investment of your time.

I learned this again when I told my Mastermind clients that they could leave me voice messages and I would respond via a messaging app. It didn't take me long to figure out that I'd made a big mistake.

My clients would often send eight- or nine-minute voice messages that I would then have to listen and reply back to. Pretty soon, just listening and responding to all their messages was taking up half of my day!

Within a matter of days, I realized this was going to be a problem. I had said yes to giving away too much of my own time, and it was clearly going to hurt my output and focus in short order.

To fix the mistake, I put a maximum of two minutes on all audio messages sent to me. I also have two phones now—one for personal use and one for coaching clients. My clients know I only work Monday through Thursday and that as soon as I'm done with work, I leave that phone in my office and don't look at it again until Monday morning.

Sometimes clients have issues come up during the weekend and leave messages during that time. But I don't check them until the next week. They are free to leave something on my "desk" over the weekend, and because I have the two phones, I'm not tempted to check it.

This decision has drastically brought down the amount of time I spend on my phone and has made responding to messages one of my favorite tasks. It's a meaningful way to connect with clients, and I do it every morning. But because I've put some boundaries around this activity, it's not something I resent or feel frustrated by.

I found this rule also had another surprising benefit. It meant my clients became more concise about their problems and the requests they made of me. A lot of the time, they discovered that they already *had* the answers to questions they were asking.

As a result of this simple boundary, our work relationship became a lot more productive and a lot more successful. It might sound crazy, but by limiting my time and availability to clients, I actually *increased* the value of the experience.

Time is our most valuable commodity, more important than money. You can spend or lose money, and there's always the opportunity to make it back. But that's not the case with time. Long-haul leaders know how valuable their time is and fight to protect it.

What you say yes to—that is, what you are committing your time to—had better be worth the cost.

NO AGENDA, NO MEETING

When I ran the call center in the Philippines, our team would hold weekly management meetings with about ten to fifteen people in the room.

The ritual began as a sit-down "chat" each week with the hope of giving everyone time to bring their problems to the table, ensuring transparency among different departments and creating a space for the management team to collaborate. We even had snacks and a coffee station.

It sounded like a great idea, and everyone enjoyed the snacks, of course. But it ended up taking an hour each week and just wasn't necessary. The fact was that we should've been able to talk through the agenda much faster. There would often be things that we didn't get to cover because I had another meeting or a client call to get to. We had to make things more efficient or keep suffering the consequences.

I'm sure you can think of similar situations in your own life. Unnecessary meetings. Pointless tasks on your to-do lists. Emails you don't need to respond to. All these things take time away from what you could be doing. And yet, so many of us keep doing them.

CEOs reportedly spend up to 72 percent of their total work time in an average of thirty-seven meetings per week. Thirty-seven! After years of putting better meeting protocols in place, I find this mind-boggling.

But . . . I get it.

This is the reality for many of my friends, peers, and even clients. We can't always control what we are asked to do at work, of course, and every life has its own set of obligations and responsibilities. But we need to reconsider what we are committing our time to and what it's really costing us.

Most people agree that meetings are ineffective and unproductive. And they come at the expense of time we could have spent on deeper work or rest. Not only that, but scheduling too many meetings back-to-back has been proven to result in lower levels of engagement and higher stress for everyone involved.

Clearly meetings are an important area where a little more intentionality can go a long way. So that's just what we put in place when I realized our weekly management meetings at the call center just weren't producing the desired effect.

To fix the problem, I established a few new boundaries.

First, everyone had to complete an online agenda form prior to the meeting, listing what they wanted to discuss. If they didn't have anything, they didn't submit the form. But team members who turned up without submitting the form were not allowed to bring up anything in the meeting.

We also got rid of the coffee and snacks and put a twenty-minute time limit on the meeting. This immediately cut down on a lot of the socializing and forced everyone to be more focused. We already had plenty of opportunities for social-izing and other "watercooler" spaces in the office. We didn't need a meeting to do that. I loved seeing everyone on the team getting close and enjoying each other's company, but I really needed our weekly meetings to be efficient. We needed to stay focused on problem solving and essential communications. So we axed all the chitchat and snacking and got down to business.

The last change was the most revolutionary.

We removed all the chairs from the conference room. This forced everyone to stand during the meetings, which ensured nobody talked too much. After that big change, the average time of the meeting was cut even further to fifteen minutes.

To everyone's surprise, we were still able to accomplish the same things, or more, in a fraction of the time the meetings were taking just a few weeks before. We never went back.

Today, my team has similar rules, even though most of our meetings happen online. Meetings are still limited to twenty minutes, and everyone has to submit their agenda ahead of time. If you've ever met with me, you'll hear me at some point say, "No agenda, no meeting."

There are lots of ways to make meetings more productive, but none of them work if you don't have a clear plan, including desired outcomes, important points of discussion, and key questions or problems that need to be addressed.

At the end of each meeting, we finish up with a recap of the most important points discussed and any action items or follow-up needed, along with who is responsible for what. This is another way I make sure not just my own but all my employees' time is spent wisely on tasks and conversations that will make a difference.

Since we started doing this, I found that our meetings (even virtual ones) have become more productive, efficient, and enjoyable. When everyone has clarity around the purpose of a discussion, knows how they can contribute, and has had time to think about their ideas, it's amazing what you can do in just twenty minutes.

THE CASE FOR SABBATICALS

One of the most transformative practices I've adopted in my career—for both my work and my personal lives—has been taking an annual sabbatical.

Every summer, I disappear for a month (or more), leaving my business in the hands of my trusted team so that I can refocus on what's really important, realign my perspective, and recharge my batteries.

Sabbaticals can take different forms, of course, but they're usually paid extended leaves that allow you to pursue a personal interest, hobby, research project, or volunteer opportunity for a cause that's important to you.

My sabbatical has become an essential part of my annual planning and something my family looks forward to every year. Everyone knows that the sabbatical will be a time for us all to get away and get more of what we've been missing while living our everyday lives. It's a time to disconnect from daily rhythms and reconnect with each other and ourselves.

When I tell clients about this practice, many think I'm crazy. The first thing I hear is, "That would never work for me." You might be thinking the same. But we have to remember that one of the unique benefits of being a leader is that we have more control and agency than most. Of course, with those privileges comes a lot of responsibility. But in my view, it's worth it.

You and I have a say over what our lives look like. We can't control everything, but most of us have more autonomy and power than we think. The truth is that you can't afford to keep going the way you've been going. Something has to change. You have to occasionally step back, unplug, and focus on what matters most.

Most leaders lack real time away from their work and career. Many of us feel stuck because it's so hard to take time off. We often feel guilty for stepping away for a long weekend. I know I've struggled with that in the past and hear many of my clients say the same. This struggle to unplug, I believe, is one of the biggest problems facing business leaders today.

New York Times bestselling author Kirsten Powers writes about our obsession with productivity, saying, "It used to be considered just normal behavior to not work on the weekend. Now, not checking work-related emails or responding to work calls (also known as not working on your day off) is in the same category as staying in your pajamas all day."

If that's how most of us view not working on the weekends, then the thought of taking an entire month or more off? As Jimmy "The Gent" Conway from *Goodfellas* would say, "Fuhgeddaboutit."

Working too much is common, but that doesn't mean it's good. Extended time for rest should be the standard, not the exception. If you're like most entrepreneurs, though, you rarely reward yourself for the good work you're doing. You just worry about what you have left to do. You measure the gap, not the gain. And if you do that for long enough, your whole world will start to crumble.

If we don't take time away to reflect on how far we've come, we'll never enjoy where we are.

I see with clients that their workloads become more complex over time. Scope creep happens all too fast without purposeful pauses to reflect and assess whether what we're doing aligns with our intentions. We end up doing admin work that we could have easily delegated or abandoned.

Leaders especially have a hard time letting go of tasks they may or may not be best suited to handle. And when we do that, everything suffers.

Regular sabbaticals are not just a nice idea for the 1 percent. They're becoming an increasingly recognized response to the persistent burnout that plagues our culture. And there's real research behind it.

One study found that people who take sabbaticals report coming back feeling significantly more confident and refreshed. They set better boundaries around their time and focus more on tasks and projects that are personally meaningful to them.

The Sabbatical Project, an organization dedicated to researching the impact of sabbaticals, has found that for many people, these long breaks amount to "peak experiences." The experiences people have are often life-changing.

There are also benefits for companies and businesses who encourage their employees to take time off. Sabbaticals lead to improved well-being and are a great strategy for employee retention, especially in industries where workers are chronically overwhelmed. They can also spark renewed energy, focus, and creativity when team members come back to work.

For employees who use their time away to develop new skills, a company can clearly benefit.

If you're considering offering sabbaticals to your employees, remember that this must be planned carefully, with fair policies that provide the same benefits to all employees and with clear guidelines.

Companies that offer sabbaticals will bear the responsibility for making sure work is covered while an employee is on leave. This can be done by hiring temps, redistributing tasks, setting up automated systems, and establishing clear decision-making processes. Adobe, Clif Bar, Hubspot, Microsoft, and even McDonald's offer extended leave to employees who have been with the company for a certain number of years, usually five to ten.

If you're a business owner, you might consider whether this could improve results for your company—and certainly for yourself! Personally, I've found that prolonged time off gives me more mental freedom and allows me to reset, recalibrate, and renew my energy. It gives me time to focus on my passions and hobbies.

Leaders tend to have a variety of interests. But you can't enjoy the benefits of those interests if you don't set aside intentional time to pursue them. Taking a sabbatical gives my wife and me time to revisit our business plans and LifeOS. It allows us to review our goals, reconnect with our intentions, and set new ones, if needed. If you're interested in taking a sabbatical but not quite sure how to get started, let me help you make a plan to make your time off as empowering and transformative as it can be.

PLANNING YOUR SABBATICAL

Before you start imagining yourself on a beach with a daiquiri, let's get practical. First, set some goals for how you want to spend your time off. And be as clear as possible about your intentions for your sabbatical. The Sabbatical Project has discovered that these long breaks typically fall into one of three types:

+ "Working holidays" are defined as dedicated time away to work on a passion project—with plenty of rest as well.
+ "Free dives" are sabbaticals framed around travel or exploration to enjoy a new place or experience.
+ "Quests" begin with an intense period of recovery and end with a drastic realignment of work and values. Questers tend to come back from sabbaticals ready to make some major changes in their lives.

Reading these, you might immediately know which sabbatical would be right for you, or you may need some time to think about it. To begin, consider the following questions in these areas:

+ **Recovery:** What areas of life do you need a break from? What needs healing or improvement?
+ **Dreams:** What's on your bucket list that you haven't achieved? Is there an experience you know would be powerful for you or help you reach a goal?
+ **Reset:** What priorities do you need to reevaluate? Perhaps you've been neglecting time with family or ignoring a particular passion project. Now is the time to realign with those priorities and make room for them.

For each of these categories, identify some outcomes you'd like to achieve by the end of your time away.

And then, once you're clear about your goals, it's time to decide how to make it all happen. Here's what that looks like.

1. Decide When

Should you go when work is slow or take a break during the busy season? If your job has seasonal rhythms, it might make sense to tie your sabbatical to a slow time.

Or, depending on your goals, you may need a time of recovery or to take a quest just when things are feeling the most hectic. Your family's schedules—such as school vacations and/or busy/slow seasons in your partner's work—should be factored into your thinking as well.

2. Decide Where

What places allow you to truly be yourself? I love being out in nature, seeing the trees and wide open skies. I want to feel dirt beneath my feet. That's where I do my best thinking and reflecting.

Which is why on our yearly sabbatical we often end up in the countryside, somewhere far away from the hustle and bustle of daily life. I need rolling water, birds chirping in the morning, and the peace of the outdoors to truly decompress and reconnect with myself and my priorities.

Of course, I know some who need the opposite, who get energized by a big city or want to sign up for some adventure with friends and fellow questers. Whatever your preference, it is important to get away during your sabbatical, at least for part of it.

This doesn't mean you have to travel the world or anything, but consider a camping trip, a few nights in a nearby hotel, or a very intentional staycation to change up the pace of your daily life and get yourself out of your typical rhythm. The point of the sabbatical is to reassess and realign, so make sure you're giving yourself space to do just that.

3. Decide How Much

Sabbaticals have two costs: time and money. That's it.

The most important cost to consider, of course, is the time. Sabbaticals can range from one to several months, depending on your goals. I typically take a sabbatical each year, and the month of August is *usually* enough time for my family and me to recharge and reconnect. If your goal is to write a book or travel the world, you may need more time.

There's no right or wrong here. Whatever the length of time, you have to plan for it. Get approval from HR if need be, talk to your team and colleagues about your goals, and ask what they need from you in order to continue to be successful during your absence. It may require putting new systems or decision-making protocols in place so that work can continue while you're away. Often sabbaticals bring hidden benefits of getting us to offload work we should never have been doing in the first place.

Once you know the details, total up the cost and make that your savings goal. There are also organizations that provide scholarships or grants for sabbaticals as well.

When my wife and I start planning our sabbatical, which we always do directly after the current one so that we know what we're doing the next year, we take into account three factors:

1. **The place:** Where do we want to go? Where have we not visited before? Where have we visited that we enjoyed so much we want to return?
2. **The kids:** Sabbaticals on your own or with your spouse will look a lot different from sabbaticals with children involved! Wherever we end up going must offer a good number of experiences for the kids to enjoy.
3. **The budget:** We're in a good spot financially and don't have to worry too much about pinching

pennies these days. But we still take regular trips as a family throughout the year, as well as our monthlong sabbatical, so we have to pay attention to what we're spending. A sabbatical does not have to be a luxurious vacation. More importantly, it's simply an opportunity to reset your priorities and realign your life around what matters most to you.

To help you plan your sabbatical, we have some resources and downloadable planning tools available at longhaulleader.com/resources.

DON'T CALL IT A COMEBACK

In July 2021 Simone Biles, the most decorated gymnast in history, made a shocking decision right before her final events at the Tokyo Olympics. She was pulling out.

It was a huge blow to the US gymnastics team and to fans around the world. But she did it anyway. Things hadn't been going well for Biles for a while. The world was still coming out of the COVID-19 pandemic. In fact, the Olympics had been postponed from the year before, and even when they resumed in 2021, no one was allowed to attend the games in person.

Instead, 1,000 cameras followed Biles and other Olympians everywhere they went. The organizers of the games instituted strict policies to shield athletes from exposure to potential viruses, which was a blessing and a curse. Through it all, the competitors were being analyzed and judged by both Olympic staff and the public via social media. All were feeling the pressure.

Biles qualified for six final events and was expected to come home with multiple gold medals. But after one performance, she told her trainer, "I don't want to do it. I'm done."

What happened?

In the middle of one of her signature moves, the 2.5 twisting Yurchenko vault, Biles lost track of where she was in the air. It was a classic case of what gymnasts call "the twisties," a stress-induced condition that renders an athlete completely incapable of performing even the most routine moves.

In a post on Instagram, she described the experience as "literally can not tell up from down . . . Not having an inch of control over your body. What's even scarier is since I have no idea where I am in the air I also have NO idea how I'm going to land. Or what I'm going to land on."

She somehow landed safely, but the experience was enough to convince Simone Biles that she needed to stop. For the next two years, she didn't compete in gymnastics, and many feared it was the end of her career.

During that time, though, she was busy. Biles went to therapy. She made guest appearances on TV shows. Snapchat made a limited series about her, showcasing her taking on a number of interesting hobbies like cooking, beekeeping, and DJ-ing. She gave countless interviews and posted on Instagram about her mental health, becoming a spokesperson for a cause she cared deeply about. She married Green Bay Packers safety Jonathan Owens, and they built a house together. Her gymnastics training continued.

Technically Simone Biles was on a break, but you couldn't say she was doing *less*. The only thing she was doing "less" of was competing.

In October 2023, she showed the world that her time away hadn't weakened her. She smashed the competition at the USA Gymnastics National Championships, taking home her eighth all-around title. Far from diminishing her or holding her back, Biles's time away had made her even stronger and more focused, putting her at the top of her game.

The following year, she returned to the Olympics in Paris and continued her winning streak, becoming the most decorated gymnast in history.

Some called it a comeback. But that's not right. It was an intentional step away to refuel, retrain, and reset her life around the right priorities. In an article for *NBC News*, Biles said, "I think I have to take care of myself a little bit more and listen to my body and make sure that I'm making time for the important things in life."

Stepping away was necessary for Biles to break the cycle of stress in a field known for overwork, overtraining, and the pain that often results from the two. She took some time to address old wounds and traumas so that she could emerge from her sabbatical with more peace, clearer priorities, and stronger habits. And we can do the same.

I don't care who you are. Staying busy with the wrong stuff will run anyone down, including an Olympian! Which is why we need to press pause once in a while and reassess our priorities. How else will we get the perspective we need to stay in this game for the long haul?

It's not activity, after all, that stresses a person out. It's the kind of idle busyness that consumes most of our lives. When we start using our time more wisely, focusing on the right priorities with the right intentions, we'll be better able to lead. We need to fill our lives with what will energize us and help us continue being better versions of ourselves.

CHAPTER 5

Upgrade Your Batteries

Long-haul leaders protect their energy.

F or many years while we were living in the Philippines, Erz and I talked about moving to the United Kingdom. For me, it would be a return home. For her, it would mean starting over. We loved the idea of getting a place in the countryside where our kids could grow up safely with plenty of room to run around outdoors.

We had a comfortable life in the Philippines, but we knew it wasn't what we ultimately wanted. So in January 2017, we found a property in the English countryside and decided it was time to make the move. It was a beautiful place, a historic house registered with the English Heritage association, but it needed significant restoration to make it livable. Nonetheless, we were committed to making it happen.

What we thought would be a six- to eight-month project ended up taking well over a year. And for most of that time, I was managing it all from the Philippines. Working with architects, project managers, and material suppliers from across the globe was a logistical nightmare. On top of that, we had our daughter Cassie during that time, and our son Charlie was a rambunctious little boy—like most little boys often are. It took all my energy just to keep the engines of business, family, and home renovations running smoothly.

By the time we moved in, in September 2018, I was exhausted. But in many ways, the work was just beginning. I had to reestablish myself and my business in the United Kingdom. We had to find Charlie a new school and buy a car to run our kids around. Erz had left behind all her family and friends in the Philippines to start a new life and was already feeling homesick. And none of us were sleeping well with a ten-month-old in the house. Combine all that with the fact that we were preparing to host our second Youpreneur Summit in London just two months later—an event that had already sold out—and it was safe to say we were up against it!

This period was one of the most stressful times in our family's life, and I'd be lying if I said there weren't a number of times when we questioned whether we had made the right choice moving to the United Kingdom. It took us a solid year to get our feet back under us and feel like we were settled. Then the pandemic hit, turning our world upside down once again. Looking back, it's easy to see how I arrived at the state of near burnout I shared in the introduction.

When you're living in survival mode for so long, all your physical, mental, and emotional resources are focused on simply getting through each day. It's hard to take care of yourself under those circumstances, a bit like running an electric car down and then charging it for a few minutes, then trying to drive it again. You might get it out of the garage but likely won't go very far!

That's how I felt every morning.

I was sleeping poorly. My body was craving quick hits of energy, so I ate terribly. I felt like crap (from all the junk I was eating and sleep I wasn't getting) and didn't have the time or energy to exercise. I also wasn't making space for hobbies and other activities I loved, because I just felt like I didn't have enough time. Overall, I felt drained, depleted, and downright depressed. No wonder it was so difficult to face my work—I was beyond stressed!

Stress is one of the greatest enemies we face in modern life—seriously. It is the most likely thing in your life to destroy good relationships, drain your happiness, and even kill you if you're not careful. And the fact is, none of us is equipped to handle the amount of stress we are forced to meet on a daily basis. It's just so much, and most of us are struggling to keep up.

But the trick isn't to avoid stress. That would be nice but isn't an option. Stress is inevitable for much of life, so we have to prepare ourselves to handle it *without* letting it take us down. For that, we can't continuously just "recharge our batteries." Taking a sabbatical or managing our time better is good, of course, but it can't change everything. To do that, you have to overhaul your whole life and how you approach every task. It's not enough to just recharge the batteries. You have to upgrade them.

LIVING IN A STATE OF CONSTANT STRESS

When we keep using the same old batteries, they're bound to run down. If you're living in a state of constant stress, you're doing just that—never taking the time to fully recharge, never stepping back far enough to see the big picture. As a result, you can't perform at your highest level. And when this happens, you have no idea what you are depriving the world of.

Author and columnist Kirsten Powers has dealt with the effects of prolonged stress and seen the challenges of ignoring the warning signs. Powers herself was diagnosed with an immune disease as a result of chronic stress. The doctor who diagnosed her told her to take a minimum of six months off from work.

"If you don't do this," he said, "one day you will lie down and not be able to get up again."

At first, Powers didn't listen. She kept working—she had bills to pay, after all—and allowed the stress to build. Eventually, though, she had to take charge of her health. Even after she made profound changes, the damage would take years to undo. "Think of how many years it took to create the problem," a coach told her. "It won't be undone with a month of rest in another locale."

Most of us are like Powers. We know we have a problem. Some of us have even experienced the warning signs of living under too much stress. Aches and pains that don't go away no matter what pills you take or treatments you undergo. An inability to make good decisions (or any decision at all!). Restless sleep. Disturbing dreams. The recurrence of bad habits like grinding your teeth or biting your nails. Stress can reveal itself in a number of subtle and not-so-subtle ways. When this happens, we need to pay attention.

While the stressors can vary, our response to stress never changes. Or, rather, our *lack* of response. Allow me to explain. Stress is a signal to our bodies that we aren't safe. When we don't feel safe, our bodies respond to save energy for what we need the most: survival.

Here's how it happens.

You're living your life, perfectly happy (or at least stable and consistent). And then stress shows up in the form of your mother-in-law popping in for a surprise visit. Or maybe it's a late-night text from your boss who's delivering bad news. It doesn't matter what it is. Your brain reacts the same way. The part that scans for trouble springs into action: *Danger! Danger!* And just like that, your sympathetic nervous system is engaged, flooding the body with cortisol and shutting down all unnecessary biological functions.

Your heart rate increases. Your digestion slows down. And your immune system hits the "snooze" button while you address the danger. It's also hard to sleep in this state, because who has time to rest when there's a tiger chasing you? Long-term thinking and executive functioning decrease in such a stressed state. Everything is focused on addressing the threat.

This is not necessarily a bad thing. If you're trying to escape the clutches of a hungry animal, cortisol can be your friend. But most of us aren't doing that on any given day. Instead, our bodies are attempting to use the same energy our ancestors used to outrun predators to protect us from something we *can't* flee: the daily challenges of work, family, and life. So our bodies live in a constant state of anxiety, hijacked by cortisol, unable to perform many of the functions we need for long-term thriving.

When this happens, not only are we cheated out of a happier, more productive, and more energetic future, but we're also *doomed* to something worse. Chronic stress has been linked to heart disease, cancer, stroke, diabetes, Alzheimer's, lung disease, kidney disease, and liver disease—eight of the top ten causes of death in the United States. It really can kill you.

So we need to learn to adapt to the daily realities of stress. We can't wish away our situations or completely change our biology, but we can find new ways to get more of the energy needed to do what matters most.

HOW TO CREATE MORE ENERGY

Continuing to show up for the people and things that matter most is no short order, of course. It demands a lot. To operate at our highest level—to be a true long-haul leader—we have to increase our capacity, which won't just happen by accident. If you want more energy, you're going to need to create it.

Think of an iPhone. Every time a new one comes out, Apple focuses on making two major improvements. First, it improves the camera (everyone always wants a better camera, after all). Second, it enhances the battery life. I think there's something to be said about making the same kind of enhancement in your own life. Upgrade the way you take care of yourself, and you'll have more of the energy you need. The following strategies can help you do just that.

Listen to Your Body

You probably already know when you're stressed. But sometimes people trick themselves into thinking they're fine without realizing how much stress is really affecting them. The first sign of stress is in the body. A tooth starts to ache. You feel an unexpected pain in your back. Certain foods that never bothered you before don't seem to settle. You have bizarre dreams. You can't remember something important. The signs are there, if you would only listen.

As I've gotten better at listening to my own body, I've learned my own signs. What hits me first is brain fog. It's not that I forget things, but I find it hard to concentrate for more than fifteen minutes at a time.

If I'm trying to get through my emails, for example, I may have to read an email three or four times before the message sinks in and I can think about how to respond. If I'm in creation mode, putting together a new training or recording a batch of podcasts will take me four times as long as it normally does.

The next sign is that I start slipping back into night owl mode, where I want to stay up and watch TV late into the night. When I make a regular practice of being in bed by 10:30 every night, I can fall asleep and sleep soundly all night. But if I go to bed later than that, I toss and turn for an hour and a half and struggle all night long to get good rest.

Your signs are unique to you, of course, but they are there. You can learn to notice them too by using one of my favorite techniques: *the body scan.*

The body scan is a method for taking a mental note of the sensations in your body, things you may have been subconsciously avoiding or ignoring because you've been so focused on doing what's in front of you, tackling whatever problems have arisen throughout the day.

The beauty of the body scan is that you can do it anywhere at any time. First, get comfortable (or as comfortable as you can be). Sit or lie down. And close your eyes. Take a few deep breaths: in through the nose and out through the mouth.

Then, relax your shoulders and your jaw. Pay attention to how your breath feels entering your lungs, filling up your chest and stomach.

After that, pay attention to what you feel. Start at your toes and move to the next area of the body, asking yourself how each part feels. Your answers might change as you work your way through the body. For example:

How does my face feel?
Fine.
How does my jaw feel?
A bit stiff, actually.
What about my neck?
Okay . . . I think.
Shoulders?
Oof—definitely tense.
And so on.

With a body scan, you're on a fact-finding mission. You're not trying to judge, fix, or change anything. Imagine you're a journalist interviewing a subject, curious about what's going on. You have a vested interest in what the answer is, but try to put that aside for a moment. For now, just notice.

Over time, this becomes natural. You'll be able to scan your body and discover new information about yourself almost immediately. *My stomach's a little queasy. I wonder what's up with that?* Once you notice what's going on, you can make a plan and respond accordingly. By being proactive, you aren't just recharging your batteries—you're upgrading them, allowing yourself to operate at an even higher level.

Get Serious About Your Health

In Chapter 2, you may have already set intentions for your health as part of the LifeOS process. If so, take this opportunity to come back to those and refine them. If not, take some time to do it now. Remember the three questions:

+ What do I really want?
+ What am I willing to give up to get it?
+ What are my nonnegotiables?

I've already shared two of my nonnegotiables: my monthly deep-tissue massage and chiropractic appointments. These align with my intentions to prioritize rest and healing. But those aren't my only intentions. Sometimes I determine my intentions with the help of my doctors, who keep me informed about my ongoing health needs.

For example, my functional medicine doctor, Dr. Nicole Goode, has recommended many supplements to help with my adrenal health, sleep, and blood sugar balance. She's also suggested I go gluten-free for prolonged periods to help with fatigue and brain fog issues.

As I've taken her advice over the years, I've noticed that when I am gluten-free, I'm a lot sharper. No matter what's going on in my life, brain fog doesn't seem to come for me like it does when I'm eating pasta and pizza. Without the effects of gluten in my body, I feel energetic and productive. I don't second-guess myself as much. I love pasta and pizza, so I'm not willing to give them up permanently, but I reserve those foods for occasional treats.

I've tried to do some kind of exercise every day. One of the improvements we made to our home in England was adding a home gym on the property so I could work out more often. Over time, I've noticed that when I exercise, I feel more alert and ready to tackle the day. I feel stronger too, and at my age that's a good thing!

Exercise also helps me sleep better, which only gives me even more energy. All these physical benefits have a direct effect on my mental health too. I can switch off more easily and go deeper in my relationships at home. All in all, exercise and diet have helped me not just push myself further but actually feel like a new person.

One important key to my consistency with exercise is that I don't micromanage the process. Instead of following a strict daily regimen, I mix up my routine often so that it always feels fun and new. One day, I might use the cross-trainer. The next, I might hop on the stationary bike. Or, if I'm feeling stiff, I may just stretch out on the yoga mat or lift light weights for a while.

Having options makes going to the gym every morning feel less like a chore and more like an interesting activity. If I make it too rigorous, it becomes an obligation I want to avoid. *What do I feel like doing today?* Even that question feels more energizing than *I have to work out this morning.*

Whatever you do for physical exercise, be sure to make some of it fun so that you don't burn out on it. That's a key to not just recharging your batteries but fully upgrading them.

Create Better Boundaries

A past member of my Round Table, Tom, is an innovation consultant for some of the largest companies in the world. He told me that whenever he's feeling close to burnout, he goes back to the basics.

"For me," Tom said, "it's always the simplest stuff that works without any hesitation whatsoever. It's going to the gym. It's eating better. It's getting more sleep. It's those basic things, which don't necessarily cost any money. Sometimes they're difficult to prioritize, but you've got no choice."

Several years ago, I made the decision to stop saying yes to calls in the evening. That applied to business calls with clients as well as recreational calls with friends and family. I found that my really good friends were okay with me saying, "Sorry, mate, I'm not taking calls in the evenings. Let's find a time earlier in the day." They understood I wanted to spend this time with my kids and to relax and catch up with Erz after a long day. In fact, not only did they understand—they cheered me on!

But not everyone did.

Several people were disappointed. In some cases, we were separated by many time zones, and my new boundary seemed unfair. They were unwilling to adjust, and I had to respect that. Our relationship is no longer as close as it once was, but this experience helped clarify for me which of my friends will support the choices I'm making for my health—and which ones won't.

It was hard to stand by my boundaries and let some friendships fade, but I've had to remind myself of the upside: more time with family, which is far more precious than any other relationship. I now have deeper relationships with those who "got it." Sometimes choosing more means others will choose less, and that's their choice. Let them make it.

My good friend Phil is another good example of this. Phil is my chiropractor. Even though his daily workload is quite full with seeing four to five patients per hour, he has boundaries in place to help him avoid burnout and stay focused on meeting every patient's needs.

In the morning, Phil's assistant loads all his patients' files in order of their appointments so that he can review them first thing. Throughout the day, he works with these patients one by one, with each person's condition and unique health situation fresh in his mind. Keep in mind that this may be up to thirty patients in a day!

Once he starts welcoming patients in, Phil doesn't have much conversation with his team. If anything urgent needs to be discussed or approved, his team knows to send him a message via Slack, and he'll reply as he's available. At the end of the day, he gathers his team to review anything that came up during the day and plan out the following day's patients. Phil now takes Fridays off, so whenever he's away from the clinic, his team knows only to contact him for true emergencies. That way, he can enjoy his downtime and prioritize his rest and recovery.

Having good boundaries allows Phil to do what's best for himself without worrying about anyone else for a day. This kind of intentional investment is rare for a leader and can do wonders for your energy and motivation.

If you haven't gone on "Do Not Disturb" for an entire day—stepping away from work and family and not filling your schedule with more stuff to do—try it. Go for a hike. Take a nap. See a movie. You might be amazed at what a little fun and free time can do for you and how you return to the rest of your life feeling more energized.

Be More Mindful

Mindfulness has become more of a fad lately. Being married to a yoga instructor, you'd think I would have developed a mindfulness practice earlier on, but the truth is that for the longest time, I didn't think much of it. Now I wouldn't dare go a day without at least a few minutes of mindful practice.

Mindfulness is being completely in the present moment. It sounds easy but isn't always. Honestly, it's taken me decades to hone this critical stress-fighting skill. But it helps! And I wouldn't trade it for the world now.

My first mindfulness practice is fairly routine. Every evening, before I go to sleep, I do two things. First, I lay down on an acupressure mat. Then, while laying down on that mat, I listen to the "Daily Calm" meditation on the Calm app. By doing this, I'm conditioning my body to relax and increase my blood flow. But I'm also shutting my mind down so that I'll be able to switch off when I go to bed. I've never been able to meditate on my own, but with this nightly practice I've been able to reach a state of accepting reality and staying present.

In addition to a formal meditation practice, you can also find a hobby that helps you concentrate, some fun activity that puts you into a state of flow where you don't feel like you're working or striving. That can be a form of mindfulness too.

If you've spent any time with me, you probably know that I have one major obsession in life, and that's *bonsai*. My love for bonsai started when my mum took me to see the movie *The Karate Kid* at eleven years old. I had already been a lover of all things martial arts at that point, and my personal hero was (and still is) Bruce Lee, but in that movie I saw bonsai for the first time. I was intrigued and soon after got my first bonsai book from the library.

When I turned thirteen, I got my first tree. I killed it inside six months! But that didn't deter my fascination. In my twenties, I decided to give it another try and, thankfully, had better luck. I took another break from the hobby when we lived in the Philippines and, for several years there, didn't have any trees. But when we came back to England in 2018, it didn't take me long to find that hobby again.

Now, I house approximately forty trees of varying styles, ages, and development stages. I've even built a full-blown bonsai garden on my property. It's become a big part of my life and daily routine, as the trees always need tending. For me, this hobby is the perfect "switch" I flick at the end of a long day, going out into the garden to spend time with them.

Spending time with my bonsai trees is one of my greatest joys—but it's not, as you might think, a passive joy. Tending to them is an active practice that takes immense concentration and visualization. For me, it's another form of upgrading my batteries.

Although it might look like I'm sitting staring at a tree for twenty minutes (or a few hours), I'm actually making calculations, imagining different possibilities for the tree's growth, and setting that tree up for what it will look like five years from now. It's a completely immersive flow state that has come to be my favorite form of mindfulness.

When I'm with a tree, I'm not focused on work or life worries. I'm living in the present moment. We all need practices that bring us to the present. For me, it's bonsai. For you, it might be yoga or rock climbing or even knitting. More than likely, it's a physical experience that yields immense mental benefits. As a result of these mindful practices, you can expand your capacity for going deeper in your work and living the kind of life you want instead of just the one you feel obligated to live.

ENERGY YOU HAVE IS ENERGY YOU CAN GIVE

Jenni Field, whom we already met in Chapter 2, is a business communications strategist and a longtime Round Table Mastermind member. Before she launched her own consultancy, though, Jenni worked in London doing global communications for a major corporation.

At the time, she was commuting into the city—often leaving just after 6 a.m. and returning home past 7 p.m. Although she loved her job, she realized that she didn't have any time to take care of herself or any margin to plan for emergencies.

"I remember saying to my boss," she recalled, "'I need to leave a bit earlier, because I want to get to the gym.' I was starting to realize I wasn't getting the balance I needed to have. And if there had been a crisis, I didn't have any flex in my time to support that. If something happened, I'd be working until ten or eleven at night."

When Jenni later left her corporate job to start her own business, she designed it with the flexibility she needed to spend time with the people she loved. "I wanted to find something that would allow me to build a life that I knew I wanted to lead," she told me, "that had the space in it to see my grandparents, help with my nieces, go to the gym, be outside, and build a life around those core pillars rather than the other way around."

In her new role, Jenni can prioritize two of her most important values—rest and staying present—wherever she is. Once a person's batteries get upgraded, they aren't in a constant state of feeling threatened and think a bit bigger about what could be possible in their lives. Because they've invested in the right areas and aren't burning the candle at both ends, they don't even need to hustle. Life and work can begin to feel effortless.

As Alex Charfen, an entrepreneur with over three decades of experience, said in one of his final podcast episodes, "Hustling means getting up at a good time in the morning and having a clear morning routine where you eat and you move and you hydrate and you breathe and you take care of yourself in a radically good way. You optimize your body so that by the time you sit down to work, if you're putting in six, eight, maybe even ten hours, you're putting in *optimized* hours."

Long-haul leaders know how to take care of themselves. They understand that *they* are the greatest resource they will ever have. Therefore they refuse to live in a way that runs their bodies and minds down. It's just not worth it.

When you take care of yourself, it shows. And when you don't, that also shows in how you tackle your work, how you relate to your loved ones, and how you feel in your body. It's not enough to recharge. We have to reinvest in ourselves; we have to increase our capacity.

When we upgrade our batteries, we have more energy, and this can be spent on the more important areas of life, the ones really worth it. So when it comes time to push, you're ready.

CHAPTER 6

Know When to Push

Long-haul leaders only hustle
when it's necessary.

When I was running the call center in the Philippines, a high-profile credit card processing company in New York hired us to set appointments for their sales team.

After a few months, the client told us appointments and deals kept falling through, blaming my team for setting up bad meetings. They would only pay us for the appointments that were kept, so we were at the mercy of someone else's follow-through.

This went on for a few weeks before my "Spidey sense" started tingling.

The early part of my career saw me very squarely in the "sales game," and I still see myself as a sales professional, so I know customers can get buyer's remorse. That's part of the deal. Minds change; people get sick; deals fall through. It happens. But this was happening *all the time*.

I started to get curious—and then suspicious. We were a new company, and this was one of my first real challenges as the leader. I wasn't sure what was going on, but something was up, and I had to find out what it was.

Even though I owned the company and had others managing the call center, I decided to go back and listen to the calls my team had made. I listened to several hours' worth of calls just to do my own due diligence. Our client's customers were clearly open to meeting, and all the calls I listened to had gone well. My team was doing their job. And yet our client refused to pay for over half the work we were doing.

Obviously we couldn't continue to grow the business if I allowed this to keep happening, but we also needed the income that was coming in from the client. I had a tough call to make. Should I keep our largest client, who was still paying us for *some* of the work, or stand up for my team and do what was right?

In my mind, there was no choice. I had to fire the client.

And that's just what I did. But don't congratulate me yet. It's easy to hear stories like this and praise someone's leadership, but the truth is that, at the time, it was a grueling decision. These are hard calls to make, especially in business, where you are graded not on your character but on your results. Everything, of course, has a consequence, and this decision was no different.

Our company was left in a tough spot. I had just fired our biggest client, and we only had enough money for two more payroll periods before we would have to start laying people off. At the time, we had thirty employees, and none of them were in sales. It was, once again, time to hustle.

And that's where this book got started: with me calling my team together. I told them what had happened and promised I would continue to pay them for the next two periods. Then I told them all to go home and that I would spend the next two weeks doing everything I could to make sure they still had a job by the time the money ran out. There was no work for them to do, so I let them leave. Then I got on the phone and did what I do best: *sell*.

It was a clear flip-of-the-switch moment. I remember it well. "Hustle mode" was on, and it was game time. Focused on a single goal, I was determined to sell as hard as I could to ensure my company would live to see another day.

Over the next two weeks, I did what got me started in this industry: cold-calling as fast as my fingers could dial, working through the night in the Philippines so that I could reach potential clients in the United States during the day.

It was a rough time, fueled by coffee and adrenaline. But by the end of those two weeks, I had secured five new clients of varying account sizes and was able to bring my team members back to the office and continue to pay them. I breathed a sigh of relief, as did the rest of the team. It was enough to keep us afloat for a while. I still, however, needed to find more work to grow the company and make it self-sustaining.

Hustle mode was still on.

Over the following months, with a lot of hard work and a little bit of luck, I was able to secure another major client. Learning from the client we had just fired, I flipped our business model so that new clients paid a monthly flat rate up front, instead of a commission. This based our fee on the fact that we were putting in the work, performing well, and bringing in clear deliverables, rather than on clients' subjective opinion of how good our leads were. They would no longer be able to withhold payment for no good reason.

From there the business expanded, and we were constantly filling new seats. I couldn't hire fast enough or expand office space quickly enough to keep up with the growth. Within eighteen months, we went from having a third of the fifth floor of our office building, to filling the entire floor, and then another floor after that, going from thirty employees to just under two hundred.

Thanks to a serious season of hustle, my team and I were able to save the company and set ourselves up for long-term success, building a legitimate business that continued for many, many years. What we pulled off as a result of that little sprint remains one of the proudest achievements of my career.

We all have times like this, when life asks us to step up, when we decide it's time to go to the next level. These times are rarely easy, but they are powerful motivators for growth and peak performance. They are our personal Mount Everest moments: the things you know you could accomplish if only you had the energy and courage to pull them off.

This is the stuff that long-haul leadership is made of. It's why we pace ourselves—not so we can hold back but so that when it's time to go all out, we're ready. Like any good runner, if you've been pacing yourself and giving your body what it needs, you can turn up the dial on your effort and make huge gains in short amounts of time. Often these are the most exciting and memorable times in our lives—when we really go for it.

This chapter is about how to use those hidden stores of energy to create massive change. Remember when I said, "Hustle is a season, not a lifestyle"? We will be talking about when it's time to hustle. You and I have untapped potential to achieve big things in our lives. And we need to know when those times are. So let's figure out when and where we should spend our energy.

CHALLENGES ARE OPPORTUNITIES

Most of us think of "challenge" as something negative. We talk about *challenging times* in our careers or *challenges* in a marriage. There's no doubt that some challenges are not good. They're not things we would ever choose for ourselves or the people we love. But challenges can also be positive.

Some challenges are invigorating. They motivate us to push ourselves beyond the limits of what we think we can do.

They ask us to push past our current abilities and resources, to get scrappy, work hard, and problem-solve. To get more creative. That's why I see these challenges as opportunities.

Professional athletes are constantly taking on new challenges, pushing themselves to expand what they're capable of. Similarly, a person who is trying to lose weight might do things outside their comfort zone to achieve the results they want. We all need to be challenged. To flex our skills in every area of life. This is how we get better, by doing hard things.

An important aspect of challenges is that they are *time bound*. They have a starting point and an ending point. They require a burst of energy for a short time and a specific purpose. And then, there must be a time of rest after the latest sprint.

When you start to see challenges as opportunities to lean into rather than as impossible situations to shy away from, the rewards start to add up pretty quickly. It's like going to the gym and pushing yourself a little harder each time. At first nothing seems to happen. Then weeks and months go by, and you realize how strong and how fit you've gotten.

That's how challenges work too. Suddenly you discover that you can do far more than you ever thought possible.

This doesn't mean tackling difficult things is always *fun*. I wasn't, for example, having fun when I cranked out endless calls through the night in an effort to save my business. But I was completely absorbed by and engaged in what I was doing. And when it was over, I was proud of what I'd accomplished, what my work had made possible.

Challenges are really a matter of perspective. Whether we embrace the problems in front of us or run from them determines how successful we will be.

When I faced the challenge of either continuing to work with or firing a client that was fleecing us, I had to make a choice. I could view this experience as a threat, or I could see it as an opportunity. We don't always get to choose our challenges. But regardless of how they come, either by choice or circumstance, what makes them meaningful is how we respond.

We don't *have* to engage with every obstacle or problem that comes our way. But we cannot live a long-haul life if we constantly shy away from difficult things. Sometimes you have to lean in to get the gains.

HUSTLE WHEN IT MATTERS

As an entrepreneur, I never lack ideas. I have an endless stream of new businesses, new podcasts, new books, and so on that I am interested in. There is always some new project buzzing in my brain. As a respected peer, Alex Charfen (whom I mentioned in the last chapter), likes to say, "The easiest thing in the world to tell an entrepreneur to do is to hustle, to work harder, to get up earlier, to stay up later, to sacrifice more of yourself."

He's right. We don't have to be told to work more—that comes pretty naturally to most of us. But we do need to know *when* it makes sense to press the gas and when to take a break. Discerning that difference is not always easy, but it is crucial to being a long-haul leader.

Personally, I'm in a season of life where I'm less interested in taking on big challenges—which is, ironically, a challenge for me. Sometimes it takes as much discipline to hold yourself *back* as it does to push forward. As someone who has lived and breathed the air of hustle culture for decades now, the bigger challenge for me is to stay focused on my long-term goals and not chase down some new idea just because I can.

So my current challenge is this: *How do I hold back? How do I keep first things first and ignore the latest fad or exciting idea?* The answer is simple, really. I try to stay grounded in two big priorities for my company and my life.

The first is money—though not just for the sake of more cash in the bank.

Each year, my team chooses a very specific monetary number to aim for because it allows us to continue doing our work and funding the things we care about. Then we reverse-engineer that yearly goal so we know exactly how much we need to bring in every quarter, month, and week in order to hit that number.

If we are falling behind, we know that we have to hustle to make the target. It's a good scorecard for us but also a way of maintaining some boundaries so that we don't just keep pushing for more for no good reason. But here's the important thing: once that number is hit, we don't put in any more "hustle time" to push beyond it. We don't create new money-making initiatives because we know that we have enough of what we need.

That's where the second value comes in: life outside work.

Growth always happens outside your comfort zone, and not just in business but also in your personal life. It happens when we travel and have new experiences. It happens when we keep challenging ourselves to do new things we haven't done before.

I like taking on new responsibilities and purposely putting myself in situations where I am uncomfortable so that I can learn how to manage my discomfort better. So that I can grow. This is why I take my children to new places with me. Together, we learn how to navigate unfamiliar experiences, which become cherished memories.

So the question is not whether you and I hustle but when and where and why. Hustle is a kind of rocket fuel, something you use to blast past the competition and send yourself into a whole new orbit. It is powerful and expensive, so use it wisely. But in the right doses, for the right goals, it can be magic.

THE WAY TO BE NOTHING IS TO DO NOTHING

At the end of high school, I flunked my exams. I just didn't want to put in the effort. I didn't see the point, so I didn't study or practice. Like many students, I winged it, even though I could have done better if I'd tried.

My dad knew I wasn't putting in the effort. So when I came back from my exams, I found one of my father's business cards taped to the outside of my bedroom door. On it he had written, "The way to be nothing is to do nothing."

It was extremely poetic coming from a man who was not a well-read guy but a hardworking draftsman, creating highly detailed drawings and plans for construction projects. I never saw my dad reading a book, but he knew the value of hard work and commitment.

I kept that business card in my wallet up until my late twenties. And then one evening, I lost my wallet in the back of a cab in Hong Kong. I was more upset about losing the business card with his words than I was about losing my driver's license and everything else that was in there.

I've carried his words around in my mind since then, and I think about them anytime I feel the temptation to sidestep a challenge that I know could present an opportunity to grow.

The truth, though, is that our level of commitment often makes the difference between accomplishing big goals and coasting along in life. In short, your level of commitment determines your success.

I often see my clients battling with their own lack of commitment, because they are afraid of failure or worried about what others might think. In many ways, hustle for the sake of hustling is just another way to keep ourselves distracted. But each of us has something unique to contribute, and it's important that we don't shy away from unlocking that potential.

It takes guts to go for something big for a long time, to become a true "long-haul leader."

But when you go all in on what you really care about, everything changes.

WANDERERS, STROLLERS, AND STRIDERS

I've noticed three basic levels of commitment in my clients and peers. And sometimes when you're struggling to succeed, it may be because you've found yourself in one of these zones.

First, there are the "wanderers," who are often tempted off the path to their goals.

These people get tangled in the weeds for no good reason. Their "goals" are usually more like nice ideas, but they have no real intention to accomplish them. Wanderers love ideas but shy away from hard work. This can be somewhat appropriate, especially when you're younger and still figuring out what you want to do, but as you get older and more serious about what you hope to accomplish, too much wandering can hold you back.

The second group are what I call the "strollers."

These are individuals who amble toward what they want. They've got a few things figured out, but they're not putting as much energy or as many resources toward their goals as they could be. Their energy and attention are both still sometimes sidetracked by other things that appear urgent and cause them to forget their priorities. Strollers have good intentions and want big things, but they aren't making those goals a priority.

And finally, the third group are the "striders."

These people are walking the path toward their goals with purpose and determination. They don't get distracted by other things that might lead them off course. They are clear about their intentions, single-mindedly focused on achieving them, and determined not to let anything stop them.

Granted, you can't be a strider in every area. But when you find something you are really passionate about, a goal or a cause that consumes you, you can learn from the striders of the world who are pursuing big things patiently. Sure, striders may have to hustle on occasion, but that is a choice they make willingly and consciously in service of a bigger vision. Knowing when to sprint and when to walk is an important lesson for every long-haul leader.

I often ask clients the following questions when it comes to their commitment level to a new project:

1. How much time and effort are you truly willing to dedicate to this new idea/opportunity/challenge?
2. Does it take you away from the goals you identified earlier? Or do those goals need to shift?
3. How many resources do you have at hand right now, and is this the best use of those resources?
4. What will you have to say no to in order to say yes to this?

This is how I can tell the wanderers and strollers from the striders.

And finally, I ask them to consider the support they need to take on a new challenge. I tell them to make a list of all the people who would also need to be on board in order for that thing to succeed. This can include family, staff, peers, friends, or even hired support, like a coach or consultant.

You want to only say yes to an opportunity or challenge if it takes you closer to your intentions for your life. And make sure those closest to you support your decision. They do not have to totally understand it, but they should see your commitment.

Personally, I can be committed to something for a long time, even if that means saying no to other opportunities, provided I know that I have the right support and vision. If you take a minute to listen to your own gut, I imagine you'll know what those things are for you as well. You can tell pretty quickly whether a new opportunity is a shiny object or diamond in the rough.

Remember that just because there's an opportunity in front of you, that doesn't mean you have to take it. Trust your instincts. When we learn to listen to the small voice in our heads and hearts and heed its warnings or promptings, we'll be much happier in the long run.

THE POWER OF "YET"

Sometimes fear stops us from taking on new challenges and hustling when we need to. There's always the risk that when we try something beyond our current skills, we won't be able to pull it off. We don't know how to succeed, or if we will, so we give up before we start. Failure, or rather the idea of it, takes us out before we even begin.

Carol Dweck, a researcher at Stanford, was interested in studying how people cope with failure. Early in her career, she was working with children and assigned them a series of progressively more difficult puzzles to solve.

As the puzzles got harder, she expected the children to get frustrated. But instead, something interesting happened.

As she writes in her bestselling book *Mindset: The New Psychology of Success*, "One ten-year-old boy pulled up his chair, rubbed his hands together, smacked his lips, and cried out, 'I love a challenge!'" Another boy said with glee, "You know, I was *hoping* this would be informative."

Although the puzzles were outside the boys' skill set, they didn't view them as impossible obstacles. They also didn't see themselves as failures. Instead, they had what Dweck calls a "growth mindset," which is a belief in their own abilities to learn and improve. They viewed their challenges as *opportunities* to grow.

Most of us have a growth mindset in some areas of life— usually, areas where failure has been normalized and we feel free to try things without shame, even if we don't succeed. These tend to be areas that feel like play: hobbies, pastimes, and things we happen to already be good at.

But many of us have been taught to believe our abilities have a natural "cap" on them, that there's some upper limit to our talents, knowledge, and skills. When a new challenge tests that limit, it creates a sense of panic: *Oh no, this is it! I can't go any further.* At that point, many people give up. This is what Dweck calls a "fixed mindset."

We most often experience a fixed mindset in areas of our lives where failure feels like a big risk. It's important to remember, though, that what you believe you are capable of is largely based on your environment and past experiences.

My friend and client Tom has noticed that a growth mindset is a key characteristic of all the successful business leaders he's known. For him, having a growth mindset is about making an effort to learn every day.

"My interpretation of a growth mindset," he told me, "is it's really about 'How can I learn stuff today?' Not just 'How can I do a sporadic training course,' but 'How can I learn more today, to try to fill the gap between what I'm doing and what the best people in business are doing—the ones who've really nailed it?' There's always going to be these people who are ahead, who are doing really smart stuff. So I want to know 'What can I learn from them today, in order to do my job 1 percent better tomorrow?'"

That's the perspective I encourage all my clients to adopt. How can we meet challenges as opportunities to get just 1 percent better? That's not a huge shift, is it? But if you add that up over time, the change can be massive. Many of my clients harbor secret beliefs about their abilities that keep them stuck, and this is always what holds them back. They simply don't believe they are capable of continually growing in a skill, getting better at something, for the rest of their life.

But the truth is they are. We all are. We just have to believe it.

My client Jack was on the verge of divorce. He was an incredibly talented CEO and poured all his energy into his team and the company. As a result, business was booming. He was committed to his health, exercising regularly and eating healthy food with a determination bordering on obsession.

He kept telling me he wanted to be home more with his wife and kids, that he was afraid his wife might leave him. But when I asked what he was doing to show up for his loved ones, he complained about all the other things on his plate.

I wasn't buying it.

After working with Jack for a few weeks, the truth finally came out. As it happened, he had a string of relationship failures in his past. He was waiting for his wife to abandon him because he didn't believe he was capable of maintaining a healthy and committed long-term relationship. He was desperately in love and assured me he wanted to stay married, but I could see that he had a fixed mindset in this area of his life. His biggest challenge was proving to himself that he actually *could* learn the skills he needed to maintain the marriage.

So we started small (1 percent improvement, remember?).

One day Jack canceled a client meeting and took his wife to lunch.

The next week he offered to take his sons to soccer practice so that she could do something for herself.

Then we made a list of the things Jack and his wife had done while they were still dating many years before. And over the next few months, he slowly repeated those early experiences on which they had built their relationship initially. All the while, he was building trust with himself and his wife, proving to them both that change was possible.

In her 2014 TEDx Talk, Carol Dweck spoke about the power of "yet." When we meet challenges we've never conquered before, we can choose to give up and repeat the same mistakes we've made before. Or we can choose to say that we just haven't conquered that challenge *yet*.

This is growth-mindset language. It implies that we might still learn how to do something we've never done before, as Tom did. We can always grow. We can always get better. We may not always succeed. But when we have a growth mindset, we'll always get further than we thought.

THE FREEDOM TO PURSUE A DREAM

At twelve years old, most adolescent boys are into sports: football (or "soccer," if you're from the United States), rugby, cricket, and the like. But not me. I couldn't seem to find a sport I enjoyed and could connect with friends over.

Until one day at school, our PE class got rained out, and my classmates and I were sent to the gym, which had a couple basketball hoops. For the first time in my life, I picked up a basketball and shot a free throw.

And then another, and another.

I shot a couple dozen more free throws and realized, *I quite like this.*

Soon I was playing after school every day. I joined the local YMCA and started playing there on the weekends. I fell in love with the game—I couldn't get enough of it. But one thing was missing: I needed a team to root for.

As a Londoner in the 1980s, I had no local team to follow, and we didn't have cable or satellite TV. I could only catch the highlights of NBA games from the United States on TV at 1 a.m. on Sunday mornings. My parents wouldn't let me stay up that late, so I set up the VCR to record the shows.

When I watched my first-ever recording one Sunday morning, I saw the highlights of a game between the Detroit Pistons and the Boston Celtics. I'm half Irish, so the Celtics' green jerseys and leprechaun mascot immediately appealed to me. Right then and there, I decided that I was a Celtics fan. I had no idea that they were one of the winningest teams in NBA history. I just liked the way they looked.

I've been a Celtics fan for nearly forty years now. And while writing this book, I had the opportunity to see them play. And not in just any game but, as I've already shared, in the NBA finals! The opportunity came, the timing worked, and I had the finances.

So I went, fulfilling a major bucket list item for me in the process. I wouldn't have been able to do it twenty years ago. But this freedom—the ability to drop everything and pursue something I've loved and dreamed of for a lifetime—is a reward of the long-haul lifestyle. You don't get that by just hustling all the time. This, my friend, is what you hustle for.

Because I've been managing my energy, time, and money well for a long time, I've trained up my team to be able to cover for me while I'm gone. I have the margin to pursue big dreams so that when the opportunity arises, I can act. Hustle has its place, but it's only worth the cost when it allows you to experience the best stuff in life. Yes, you need to rest and recharge, even occasionally upgrade your batteries. But sometimes you have to push. And the push—when done for the right reasons—can pay off.

Choosing to pursue the right opportunities and knowing when to hustle strategically to achieve our goals is crucial to long-haul leadership. And equally important is determining what to let go of in order to pursue these bigger dreams.

CHAPTER 7

Stay in Your Zone of Genius

Long-haul leaders focus on the right
priorities and let go of the rest.

David worked in the technology sector for a software-as-
a-service company that was developing a new productivity software. He came to me because his company
had a lot of big ideas and plans. They'd been struggling but
were ready to make significant progress on their initiatives
and break through their goals and key performance indicators
(KPIs).

I soon realized what their problem was. David and his team were constantly jumping from one idea to the next, trying to implement a marketing strategy for one product line, piloting another new product, and initiating an organizational overhaul of their internal systems. All at the same time.

Their small team was highly creative and passionate about the mission, but they had divided their attention across several different, seemingly high-priority initiatives. Every time someone had a new, exciting idea, it was added to the list of projects—a common problem I like to call "squirrel syndrome," like a dog chasing every squirrel that crosses its path.

In case you forgot, I'm an entrepreneur. I love new ideas, big goals, and exciting projects. But when you constantly jump from one new thing to the next, you may be having a lot of fun chasing squirrels, but if you keep changing directions, you won't catch any of them.

That was the case for David and his team. In spite of the excitement the whole team felt, none of their projects was getting done well. With the internal competition for resources, the team members were getting in each other's way. The opposite of what they wanted was happening. That is, obviously, a big problem in business, where we are judged by the outcome and very little else.

I'm a big believer in finishing what you start. When you're working on a project, you work it right through to completion before you start another. Having multiple competing priorities, as well as a leader whose attention is divided, can be a real liability.

Even though all the projects on David's team felt equally important *and* urgent to them, their lack of focus was crippling their efforts, taking them further from their goals.

So we decided to step back and refocus on a few new goals. The first was putting an end to "squirrel syndrome." Immediately. Together, David and I created a new framework to help him not just develop ideas but evaluate opportunities when they popped into his head, landed in his inbox, or were brought up by employees.

Using the new framework, we discussed each and every project his team was trying to manage and saw which were worth pursuing and which were not. The framework required the team to think through the purpose of each project without just committing to it.

These were the questions I asked David and his team, and I recommend you consider asking them of yourself the next time you think about starting something new:

1. What's the goal of the project?
2. Does this goal align with your mission? Does it move you closer to or further from your goals and KPIs?
3. What is the demand for this? Do other people want or need it? What information would you need to collect to validate or test the idea before moving forward?
4. What other competitors are out there, and are they filling the need sufficiently?

5. What would success look like?
6. What's the potential return on investment?
7. What resources (financing, staff, time, etc.) would be required to make this project successful?
8. Who would spearhead the idea, and what do they already have on their plate? Should other projects or initiatives be deprioritized to make room for this? If so, which ones? And what takes precedence over this new project?
9. How long will it take to begin realizing the return on investment?

After running each idea through this assessment, we realized that many were already being executed by competitors, and competing would be difficult. We nixed those immediately. But this process opened up an opportunity for further discussion about the company's value proposition and what it could offer the market that other larger companies could not.

Once we got all the company's priorities settled and made a plan for each month, we made another major change.

Every Monday morning, I asked David to email me a bulleted list of the major projects/initiatives he had worked on the previous week. We did this for three months straight. Over those months, we saw that his list became shorter and shorter. He stopped chasing squirrels and started focusing on the shorter list of projects his team was working on.

Those weekly emails helped David stay focused and ensured that the right resources were in place and that he channeled his attention and creativity into supporting his team. By the end of the three months, the company had met multiple goals and was set for long-term success.

The ability to remain committed to and focused on the most important priorities is one of the highest-leverage practices a leader can adopt. In Chapter 2, we got clear on our intentions through the LifeOS framework. But now I want to give you the tools needed to maintain your commitment to those initiatives so that you, like David, can see progress in your life and work for a long time to come.

WHY LEADERS LOSE FOCUS

Leaders aren't more prone than the average person to losing focus. That's just human nature. And it always happens with the best of intentions to try to do more, be more, and serve more. But when *leaders* lose focus, the consequences can be dire.

As we saw with David, when a leader takes their eye off the ball, the whole team suffers. Goals are missed. Actions taken in an attempt to save the company become the very actions that bring it down. And the leader is left feeling like a failure.

In leadership, the stakes are high. That means we need to delve deeper and understand the ways we are tempted to lose focus. In my mind, there are four main reasons this happens:

1. **Fear of failure:** Leaders want to avoid the appearance of struggling, which sometimes leads to playing it safe and focusing on tasks that are easy to pull off. The problem with this strategy is that easy tasks aren't always the most important or most impactful. Often these tasks could be done better by others. By not focusing on what only you can do, you deprive yourself and the world of your greatest gifts—which is the greatest failure of all, in my mind. The irony is that by trying to avoid failure, we run right toward it.

2. **Reluctance to delegate:** I've seen this for the last twenty years in every business I've led and every leader I've worked with. If you're not delegating tasks effectively, you end up spending time on activities you should not be doing. Nine times out of ten, these are done better by somebody else.

3. **Overcommitment:** This is a threat to leaders' time management and productivity. I've been guilty of it myself. Because we are responsible, we make the mistake of thinking we have to do everything ourselves. We try to handle too many tasks, juggle too many projects, and pursue too many opportunities, ultimately diluting our energy and attention. We forget that our yeses are currency, and eventually we will run out. By saying yes to one thing, we instantly say no to something else.

4. **Tendency to micromanage:** This is a temptation I've noticed particularly with entrepreneurs, because many of us are type A individuals. I've been guilty of micromanaging my teams in the past. Thankfully, not so much anymore. Micromanagers tend to hang over people's shoulders, getting in the way and muddying the team's efforts. Even when they've delegated something, these managers tend to have a hard time fully relinquishing control and trusting their people to follow through.

I see clients all the time who are overly involved in the day-to-day operations of their business. When this happens, they can't see the big picture and get caught up in the minor details. They don't end up contributing what they should. They lose sight of the job only they can do.

THE JOB ONLY YOU CAN DO

Most of us didn't get into business to spend our days worrying about its minutiae, even if we might genuinely enjoy some aspects of it.

I like graphic design and typography, but that doesn't mean I should spend hours creating logos and landing pages for every product and event my company offers. There are other people who can do that far better than I can so that I can focus on what I do best: selling my products and services.

This is what Gay Hendricks would call my "Zone of Genius," a phrase borrowed from his book *The Big Leap*. Your Zone of Genius is the sweet spot where passion, expertise, and impact come together.

And it's the term *impact* that makes the biggest difference. When you're operating within your Zone of Genius, you enjoy yourself more. Work doesn't feel like work, even when it's hard. Even when you're conquering new challenges.

In your Zone of Genius, you're able to continue working at the top of your game, unhindered by tasks that could be done better by others. You are doing, quite simply, what only you can do. And perhaps even better, you're allowing your team to do the work *only they* can do. Everyone wins when they work from their Zone of Genius.

All of us want to spend our time doing things we love that contribute to those around us. Long-haul leaders find ways to spend the *majority* of their time in their Zone of Genius. We want to try to do the same. Sadly, most leaders *don't* do this. They allow busywork—stuff any trained person could do—to pack their schedules and consume their days. As a result, their lives and their work suffer.

When I surveyed my audience of entrepreneurs and business leaders, the vast majority of them—roughly 87 percent—confessed that they were "often" or "always" working on tasks that were outside their Zone of Genius. Clearly this is an area where most of us could be doing better. And to make that change, we have to start today.

Living in your Zone of Genius has a ripple effect in your life, spreading out to those you influence, helping everyone step into their unique areas of contribution.

TURNING THE SHIP AROUND

Many years ago, I had a client named Michelle who was passionate about her work as a business coach. Not only was she passionate; she was highly driven. She had high standards for everyone around her, but especially for herself, and put a lot of pressure on herself to perform at a high level. She wanted to hit every sales goal and collect amazing client feedback and testimonials after every project.

But Michelle was afraid to delegate, which led her to take on way too much at once. Instead of trusting others with less important tasks, she hoarded them for herself and became a bottleneck for the business. There was no way she could keep up with everything that needed to be done, so she got bogged down in a swamp of overcommitment.

She wasn't spending enough time working on her business. She didn't have enough space to think clearly about her vision for the company. Instead, she was living quarter to quarter in a feast-or-famine mindset, always focused on what was right in front of her instead of looking up to see where she was headed.

When I started working with her, we made a few changes right away. First and foremost, I asked Michelle to begin thinking longer term. To help her with this, we focused on identifying her top-priority goals for the year.

Once goals were set, we reverse-engineered them into a quarterly focus for the next ninety days. Every quarter, she had something new to focus on that moved her closer to where she wanted to be in twelve months.

We also took note of Michelle's strengths and weaknesses. It became obvious to her that the administrative tasks she was doing—like scheduling appointments with clients, sending follow-ups, and troubleshooting minor issues—were eating up most of her time and distracting her from doing what she really loved.

Michelle's Zone of Genius was identifying the problems underlying her clients' business struggles and creating simple, easy-to-follow pathways to solutions that worked. She was also brilliant at forming relationships with them. Her support gave them the confidence they needed to make changes and see positive results. Nobody else could do that. Only her. And yet she spent very little of her time working on this every day.

Michelle learned how to delegate administrative tasks to virtual assistants so that she could focus her attention and energy on client relationships and support. After doing this, she felt an immediate sense of relief, knowing she no longer had to worry about those tasks.

At first, it was hard to trust these things would be done well. But with some encouragement and experimenting, Michelle soon saw the benefits of delegating.

Lastly, we reassessed her schedule. Remember: if things don't get scheduled, they don't get done. Right away, we added in one hour of white space in the middle of Michelle's workday. This scared her at first, but after a week of taking a break each day, she came to love it.

Michelle realized just how important it was to have white space on her calendar so she could spend time resting or pursuing something of interest. After her breaks, she felt refreshed and ready to dive back into her work.

It's amazing what a little recalibration can do. Even if you feel absolutely "lost at sea" and completely overwhelmed by stress, your never-ending to-do list, and the bills that just keep coming, there is hope. It's never too late to right the ship.

FINDING YOUR ZONE OF GENIUS

When you hear the phrase "Zone of Genius," maybe something immediately comes to mind—something you love, something you're good at, something that contributes to the world. But sometimes we get so caught up in the little things of life that we have a hard time remembering what we used to enjoy.

A brainstorming exercise I use with clients helps you reconnect to what you love. I call it "The Three Lists to Freedom." It's a process of elimination to help leaders cull unnecessary tasks from their to-do list, and it works very simply. Just get out a blank piece of paper and draw two lines down it, creating three columns.

In Column 1, list all the tasks you *hate* but that still need doing for the health of your business. For me, this is things like filing taxes, running payroll, searching for hotels when traveling, booking flights, and scheduling appointments.

In Column 2, list all the things you don't necessarily dislike but aren't particularly good at. These are the things you struggle with, that leave you feeling drained or unfulfilled to a certain degree. For me, these are tasks like running my Facebook ad account or creating new slide decks for speaking engagements. Sure, I could do them, but I'd much rather delegate them to someone else.

In Column 3, list all the things that you might enjoy—you might even be quite good at them—but shouldn't be doing as a business owner or leader. These are tasks that distract you from your Zone of Genius. For me, these tasks are graphic design and writing copy. I can do those tasks, and I'm good at them, but I know my time is better spent on things that move the business forward. Besides, by giving these tasks to some of my team members, I'm giving them the opportunity to develop their skills and lean into their own Zones of Genius.

Any tasks that end up on one of these lists should be delegated to someone else on your team, outsourced to others who can support you, or potentially just deleted entirely. This is the only way you get to your Zone of Genius.

Handing the tasks on these lists off to people who can do them better helps me recognize where my limitations are. It also reminds me to focus my time, energy, and efforts on

The 3 Lists to Freedom

Tasks I Hate	Tasks I Struggle With	Tasks That Distract

the things that only *I* can do—which bring me the most ful-fillment, anyway. But how, exactly, do you identify the list of tasks you *should* be doing?

It's called your Zone of Genius for a reason—because this is where you thrive. So let's define what that is for you. If you were one of my clients, here's what I'd ask you:

1. **What are you really good at?** I mean, what's your superpower? What do people come to you for help with on a regular basis?
2. **What are you selling?** What's your mission? What do you believe will change the world?

Put these two together, and you've got your Zone of Genius. At the intersection of your unique skill set and other people's needs, you'll find your area of greatest contribution. For example, a superpower of mine is bringing great people together so they can collaborate and learn from each other. Whether it's through online programs or live events, I'm great at creating the right teams and partnerships to get things done.

And if that's what I'm passionate about and excel at, the question is *How can I attach that to something I already do?* When I started asking myself this question, I came up with the idea of the Round Table Mastermind. I'd been looking for something like it for a while. I wanted to join a group of six- and seven-figure entrepreneurs in the "expert business" niche—folks who wanted to build a profitable business around their expertise and experience. I just couldn't find one, so I ended up creating one for myself and invited others to join.

In this intimate mentoring program, not only do I bring the right people together but I'm also in a position where I can help them collaborate, learn from each other, and keep one another accountable. Over and over again, I hear clients say things like "I don't know how you do it, but these are exactly the right people I need!" I've seen many new fantastic products and services created in the Round Table Mastermind—all because the right people were in the room. And I was honored to bring them together.

That's my genius. What's *yours*?

WATCH FOR THESE SIGNS OF BURNOUT

If you find yourself feeling exhausted, demoralized, and unmotivated in your work, it could be that you're not taking care of your energy and upgrading your batteries. But it could also be a sign that you're doing the wrong work.

One of my Round Table Mastermind members, Joana Galvao, is the cofounder of Gif Design Studios in Portugal. They've worked with leaders and companies across the globe to provide world-class branding and design services, creating some iconic designs in the online space.

Joana has always been intentional about listening to her body and taking care of her health, but that doesn't mean she hasn't at times felt depleted and on the edge of burnout. She told me:

Because I've been aware of listening to my body and taking good care of what I eat and how I move, whenever my body gives me signs of burnout, it's more because of a misalignment with the work that I'm doing or how I'm approaching work—rather than my habits.

So there are a couple of things that I'll go through if I'm feeling like rubbish and it's, say, the third day this week. Did I sleep enough hours? Check. Okay, did I eat well? Check. Did I move my body? Check. Did I work less than eight hours? Have I spent time with my kids? Have I seen friends? Okay, if I'm able to check all those boxes and I still feel miserable, then it's a misalignment.

Burnout can happen not only if you're not taking care of yourself but if you're feeling resentful or stressed because you're spending time doing work you know isn't in your Zone of Genius.

There have been times when Joana has felt like quitting or giving up, and it was never because she hated her job. It was because she was spending too much time on aspects of her work that were not her unique areas of contribution.

"I'm good at understanding clients' visions and translating that into design," she said, "and I'm good at making things beautiful during creative direction. But as an agency owner, I was merely juggling cash flow, managing people, and overseeing projects. And that isn't my Zone of Genius, and so on top of having an unhappy team and unhappy clients, I found myself wanting to quit or sell the agency."

For Joana, the key to her success has been gathering the right team members around her so that she can stay involved in the creative process that brings her joy while still achieving the best results for her clients and her team.

SAYING NO IS A SIGN OF RESPECT

There's *always* more we could be doing. Always a new idea, new project, new task we could justify investing our time and attention in. But just because we can do something doesn't mean we should. When you feel fatigued, discouraged, or frustrated, that can be a sign that you're doing some things you shouldn't. And as is often the case, the most difficult boundaries you have to set are the ones with yourself.

In Chapter 2, I talked about how your yeses are valuable. You should give them out sparingly. But if you think about it, your nos are valuable too. After all, they make the yeses possible. So we have to get better at saying no if we want to say yes to the things that really deserve it.

This is what setting boundaries is all about. Boundaries ultimately come from an innate sense of respect for ourselves and our work. Only when I felt, deep down, that I needed to honor myself and my Zone of Genius did I have an easier time making and sticking to my boundaries.

You have to realize that you aren't saying no to something to be mean or selfish but so that you can say yes to what only you can do. In a way, it's the most selfless thing you can do.

Even though remaining in your Zone of Genius may mean you're turning down projects and opportunities, this is easier when you do it out of respect for the work you're doing and the commitments you've already made. I know that when I say no, the rewards of more energy, more time, and more fun are worth the temporary pain of disappointing someone.

Author and wellness expert Yasmine Cheyenne has a lot of experience with setting boundaries. On an episode of the *Youpreneur* podcast, she shared that one of the hardest parts of doing this is helping others feel confident enough to step up when the leader is stepping back. Here's what she told me:

> It takes time for you to teach people how you're going to be showing up when you've been doing this previous behavior longer than you have been setting these new boundaries with everyone. So it's going to take consistency, just like it would in your business. Reaffirming with people that "Yes, I know that I would have done this before. But now it's okay to do XYZ. When I say that I want you to truly take this task and do it yourself, I really mean it this time. I know before I would have micromanaged, but I really mean it." And reminding yourself that you really have to be willing to continue to show up consistently with the people

that you're setting those boundaries with, because if you don't advocate for [your boundaries], they don't exist.

Boundaries are a sign of respect—for yourself, your work, and your team. Don't neglect them.

LIVING IN THE ZONE

When you're operating in your Zone of Genius, you often have a specific goal in mind. But living in that state is a whole different ball game than simply finding it. I'm currently living in my Zone of Genius most days, working with the right clients, whom I can serve better than anyone else because of the way my business is aligned with their needs. This work taps into my unique skill set as a connector and leader, and I absolutely love it.

I also have other businesses that are practically running themselves and continuing to bring in revenue. They don't need my attention day to day because I've got an incredible team in place to run them. Combine this with the fact that I invest in and advise a number of startups, and I feel empowered and energized by the work I do. It's taken a long time to get here, but I'm so glad this is my life.

The more I've leaned into my Zone of Genius, instead of choosing to pursue every opportunity that comes my way, the more aware I've become that the work I'm doing now is truly worthwhile. And that is one of the greatest rewards in life. By staying in my lane, I've been able to create a powerful life for myself and others. I share this not to boast but to inspire.

Finding and staying in their Zones of Genius allows leaders to last for a long time. It's easy to keep doing things you love, things that feed your soul and fill you with energy. The more we do this, the more impact we can make, and the longer we can make it.

My LifeOS framework, combining personal mastery, relationships, hobbies, and impactful work, is the driving factor behind all of this. That perfect storm of passion, purpose, and productivity fuels me every day. I'm doing it. You can too. Of course, part of that framework includes how we make a living. To live fully in our Zone of Genius, we have to put money in its proper place.

CHAPTER 8

Multiply Your Money

Long-haul leaders make their
money work for them.

F ast cars. Flying first class. VIP dinners. Back-stage
passes and luxury timepieces and almost everything
you see on Instagram. Hustle culture can look sexy.

The people who enjoy these things tend to be all about the
work it takes to get them. They love talking about how much
they "crushed it," all the late nights and early mornings they
worked, and the "100 percent commitment" it took. But rarely
do they talk about the real cost: the broken relationships, the
lost time, the gnawing sense of purposelessness that comes
with pursuing success for its own sake.

To be honest, I've done this myself more than once: buying into the hype of *more, more, more*. After a while, though, it gets old. Looks can be deceiving, after all. The entrepreneurial community glorifies big risks for big payoffs. The bigger we risk, the bigger the win, right? Extreme sacrifice always leads to extreme rewards—or so the success stories tell us. But is that always the case?

The majority of "hustlers" I know tend to associate what they have with how hard they've worked. At a certain point, though, that math just doesn't add up. Working harder can only get you so far. Eventually, you have to dig in and get strategic, gaining clarity on what matters to you, what you're willing to give for what you want, and what your nonnegotiables are. You have to get clear on your intentions. Otherwise you'll drive yourself into the ground chasing *more* when what you have might be enough.

John Mackey, cofounder of the grocery chain Whole Foods, is another example of someone who put money in its proper place. Since the beginning, Mackey has always said Whole Foods was built on the principles of health, sustainability, and fair treatment of its workers and suppliers. He even implemented a salary cap for himself and top executives to maintain equitable pay structures within the company.

That's not a small sacrifice for the most profitable grocery chain in North America, which Amazon eventually acquired for almost $14 billion. But it was a bet that clearly paid off.

Mackey's focus on core values over personal gain helped the company grow into a successful and ethical business. To this day, the customers can feel it in the products they purchase and the quality of services they receive from Whole Foods team members. My dad used to say, "Money isn't something you should worry about; it's something you should use." John Mackey is clearly doing just that. He understands something every long-haul leader eventually has to grasp: you don't chase money for itself—you use it to get more of what you want.

NOT MORE, BETTER

When you pursue money to spend it lavishly on status symbols or to capture an elusive "more," you find yourself taking shortcuts. Whatever you end up with is usually not enough. As a result, you will always be working longer hours, reaching higher, and never getting closer to satisfaction.

But if you pursue money for the right reasons—to be able to provide for yourself and those you care about, to serve others well—then you'll find it easier to maintain a healthy balance between work and the rest of life, to slow down when you need to and push ahead when you must. Money is a tool that helps us fulfill our highest and best intentions. At least it can be.

There's nothing wrong, of course, with having lots of material things and lots of money. But when the only way to get more is by putting more work in, we're missing something. I see a lot of leaders chasing easy money or the "low-hanging fruit" in their industry. As we've already discussed, these people tend to lose focus, taking themselves out of their Zones of Genius, moving further from their intentions. In some cases, this can have negative effects on their reputation. Chasing easy money as an end in itself can be the beginning of the end, because it puts most people on a short-term path to quick success instead of long-term growth.

It's not that everyone who hustles wants to take part in "get-rich-quick" schemes. But hustle by definition is a short-term game. It tends to prioritize trendy, high-risk products, services, and investments that yield bigger payouts in the short run but force us to sacrifice our health and long-term success to get there.

A 2024 *New York Times* article describes YouTuber Nate Petroski, who has gone "off grid" to live on over one hundred acres of land he purchased in West Virginia. There, he lives simply, using solar power, collecting rainwater, cooking in an outdoor kitchen, growing food in a garden, and more.

Nate documents a lot of his lifestyle online, sharing everything from reviews of lawn mowers to trips to the grocery store with his dog. He self-reports making a six-figure income and having a higher net worth than he's ever had before. But he also says, "There will be a certain point where I'm good. . . . And then I'll do the things I came out here to do: hunt more, forage more, play with the dogs more."

This is the trap of hustle. It tells you that one day you can do whatever you want so long as you start making money now. Unfortunately, this can lead to a life of doing things you don't want so that someday you can hopefully get to do what you really want. Most, however, end up getting stuck in the hustle trap and never use their hard work to live the life they want. That's a problem. We can spend our whole lives doing one thing and never actually get to what we said we were doing it for.

That's not to say that hustle, or money, is the enemy—both can be allies if we know how to use them. But we have to put these things in their place. More for the sake of more is not good enough. We have to find a way to get not just more of what we're striving for—but *better*.

Financial success is about more than how much money you make. It's how you put that money to work for you. Most people won't get rich simply by working harder. At a certain point, you can't just keep hustling more—you have to find more strategic ways to earn an income. You have to figure out how to make your money work for you. Long-haul leaders aren't just interested in making a buck; they're committed to building real wealth. And that requires more strategic thinking.

Hustlers tend to seek flashy things. Long-haul leaders know that owning material things is just one expression of wealth. Hustlers brag about how long, hard, and fast they're working. Long-haul leaders are humble about their achievements and celebrate others' successes. Hustlers ask, "How do I get the biggest payout in the shortest amount of time?" Long-haul leaders wonder, "How do I ensure I and those I love have a comfortable income for the foreseeable future?"

As you can see, it's all about the perspective you choose. Following the path of a hustler will only leave you feeling burnt out, checked out, and maybe even broke. Becoming a long-haul leader with your finances will change the money game, not just for you but for generations to come.

You can't shortcut your way to financial freedom. It takes consistent work and discipline, as well as a big-picture perspective. The best way to get to true and lasting wealth is to be a tortoise, not a hare. Slow and steady really does win the race. And it all begins with getting clear on your purpose.

WHAT DOES YOUR MONEY SAY ABOUT YOU?

When you're desperate for more, you'll do anything to get it. In life and in money, ethics matter. You can tell a lot about a leader by the way they handle their finances: what they say about money, how they use it. You can see what people value by the way they treat the people around them and where they spend their hard-earned cash.

Let's look at you, for example. Do you pay your bills on time? Do you give generously to others? Do you hold back resources others need because you can?

How you do business says a lot about *why* you do business. Actions, of course, speak louder than words. And money, quite frankly, talks the loudest. So let me ask you, Why are *you* in business? To answer that question, though, I don't want you to say anything. Show me, instead, your credit card statements, your P&L, and your checkbook. That speaks so much louder than words.

How you treat money demonstrates what you value. What is it you stand for? What is it you bring to your organization, to the people you serve? When you let a client overpay you, what does that say about your character? What about when you know the value of your product or service, but people are willing to pay more for it? Or when you believe you could talk someone into doing something that isn't good for them but would make you a ton of cash? What we do in times like these tells us who we really are.

Money should be a way for us to further our purpose in life. It ought to be something that benefits our clients and customers, our team members, and even our loved ones. But when we get caught up in the hustle game, pursuing more for the sake of more without any reason or vision, we end up losing our way. Money begins to be the driver of our decisions instead of a tool we can use.

When we do this, we can see it. Our families, customers, and employees feel what we value. When you stay late every night for a month to work for that next bonus so you can take your family on vacation, what does that say about what you really care about? There is no right answer, but we had better know why we're doing what we're doing, especially when it comes to money. To keep pursuing it is too easy otherwise.

GET SERIOUS ABOUT YOUR FINANCES

About six years ago, when my family and I had just moved back to the United Kingdom from the Philippines, I had money on my mind. We had finally finished the renovations on our home and moved into the new house. I was all-out focused on earning an income to fund our new life together.

We needed new cars. We needed to send our son to school. My youngest was just under a year old and had her own set of needs. On top of that, everywhere I looked, I saw reminders that the cost of living in the United Kingdom was drastically higher than it had been in the Philippines. Well, what did I expect moving from a developing nation in the tropics back to Europe? Everything was *way* more expensive, and it was seriously stressing me out.

I knew I needed to step up my game to make sure we had enough to meet our needs, in both the short and the long term. So I met with my financial and tax advisors, who told me that actually I was in a more comfortable financial position than I thought. But if I didn't start managing what we had more wisely, it wouldn't last very long. This was the wake-up call I needed.

Obviously, I wouldn't always be able to bring in the same level of income we had been used to, so some things had to change. Erz and I made a more aggressive plan to make our money work for us instead of constantly striving just to stay ahead. We hired the right investment managers and made some investments. Our advisors told us about opportunities we might be interested in and where we could save on unnecessary costs.

One of the best things we did was start meeting in person twice a year with our chief financial advisor. He and I are in communication throughout the year, of course, but twice a year we take an overall look at the health of the family finances.

Together, we dig into all the assets and investments we have, assess where we are in relation to our financial goals, and discuss anything that's changed. Erz and I maintain a revolving five-year plan that our advisor is aware of and gets to critique and evaluate. As a team, the three of us are regularly planning for the future while assessing where we currently are.

Having someone to point me in the right direction has been a game changer for us. Our advisor, David, has helped Erz and me understand that sometimes you've got to take a little bit out of one financial bucket and top up another one to maximize an opportunity, then level things back out again. It's not about perfect balance as much as it's about managing tension.

David has also helped us make space in our finances to pursue opportunities when they arise, while ensuring our overall financial situation continues to be stable. Working with him has been a godsend, knowing we've got someone in our corner who's looking out for us. As a result, we've become more aware of and educated about all our financial options. It's been fun and interesting to take advantage of the opportunities that have come about because of this renewed focus on our finances.

When you commit to making your money work for you, the whole game changes.

MAKING YOUR MONEY WORK FOR YOU

If you're anything like most leaders I meet, you're a hustler (maybe, like me, a recovering one!). You've worked hard for what you've earned and put in the long hours, so it's only fair you should get compensated. But how you do this makes all the difference.

Long-haul leaders work hard for their money, of course, but they don't see themselves as beholden to it. Instead they ask, "Now how can I make this money work *for* me?"

The most important part of making money work for you is having a long-term focus on diversification. You have to be careful where you invest and how. Truly great leaders aren't just focused on a quick return; they're trying to build true wealth, not just stockpile cash. Cash is important, of course, but not the only goal.

When you build a diverse portfolio across a variety of interests, you begin stacking the deck in your favor. Doing this spreads out your risk, so that as investments ebb and flow, other interests can protect the downside. So even after a bad go of it, you can still live to fight another day, which is what financial health is all about.

Long-haul leaders have the kind of relationship with money that allows them to meet their goals, fulfill their intentions, and have some fun doing it—and you can have the same.

One of the first things our advisor did was help us understand the various "buckets" in our financial life. There are three types of assets in this framework: liquid assets, illiquid assets, and real estate.

The liquid side of things, for us, is made up of five buckets. First is our pension fund.

Next is our individual savings account for compounding tax-free gains. The US equivalent would be a Roth IRA. It's just a simple retirement account that builds over time into a nice little nest egg.

After that is cash, which is used for personal allowances, savings, and short-term liquidity.

Then, there are investment funds, which provide dividends and capital gains, and alternative exposure for opportunities, such as startup and angel investing.

And finally, we have a revolving investment bond for non-income-producing assets, such as fine whisky, certain collectibles, art, and so on.

These buckets have been set up for a few reasons. First, they help me understand how the different options complement each other. Second, they allow us to be somewhat flexible with where certain allotments of savings can go and where they can be used. And third, they keep us from putting all our eggs in one basket. I really like the setup for its diversity and low risk.

To be sure, this is not my wheelhouse, so my advisor handles most of the big decisions, but I have access to the full scope of things and can make changes whenever I see fit. I share all this here not so much for you to copy any of it—you'll have to do what works for you—but so that you can start thinking of your money and assets more strategically.

In addition to the liquid side of things, there are illiquid assets, such as private shareholdings, which help create a lower rate on any capital gains. And then there's real estate, comprising both residential and commercial investment properties we have.

I may not know every intricate detail, but I have a solid grasp of the fundamentals, trust my advisors, and see progress heading in the right direction. Balancing when to dive deep and when to focus on the broader picture is essential for long-term financial success. What I really love about this side of things is that I am always learning something new.

When it comes to your own finances, you don't need to know exactly how everything works. You just need a general understanding, trust in those you've chosen to guide you, and your finger on the pulse. Knowing when to dig in and when to focus on the big picture is also part of playing the long game.

PASSIVE INCOME IS WORTH THE INVESTMENT

You don't need to be a certified financial planner to manage money smartly. You just need to know what you don't know and bring along the right people to help you understand your options. Like passive income.

A lot of people say passive income is a myth, that no matter what investments you make, you've still got to work for them. It's true to an extent. No income will ever truly be "passive." But that doesn't mean it's not worth pursuing. Long-haul leaders put high value in income where the return far exceeds the initial investment and the time it takes to manage it.

Passive income is real, and the opportunities to earn it are abundant. Let's take rental properties as an example. Real estate is one of the most successful strategies for building long-term wealth. No, it's not totally "passive," but few things actually are. That doesn't mean they aren't worth investing in.

When you buy a rental property, you almost immediately have income coming in (provided you can get the renters), but you may also have to pay a property manager and your taxes, as well as absorb the costs for home repairs and even remodeling. You have to spend the time it takes to manage these expenses, show the home, interview property managers, and more. It's not a full-time job, but it does take some work to set up.

There are, of course, occasional costs in time and money that come every month or year with the rental property, but the monthly income you receive adds up and tends to outweigh the costs. Over time, owning a rental property is usually a net-positive experience, provided you didn't invest in a bad part of town. As long as you are keeping up with the expenses, the equity in the home (in most cases) will continue to climb. That's a good investment and a great way to earn passive income long-term.

Another example is automated income earned from digital information products, like membership sites and online courses. Once you do the work and create all the content, that collection of assets can be sold over and over and over again. Yes, there's still going to be work involved. That's just the cost of doing business. You may also have to maintain a website, respond to customer questions or emails on occasion, and address potential errors with the software you're using to deliver the products.

Occasionally, with online information products, you may have to update the content to ensure it stays relevant to the audience. But there's not a month that goes by that I don't make several thousand pounds from completely automated products.

The return I make on this income far outpaces my investment in the upkeep. I pay my team to manage most of this and to tell me when something breaks or if I need to update some material. It is almost entirely passive income, and I love that I made these investments years ago and continue to reap the rewards.

BUILD SCALABLE BUSINESSES

Another way to build wealth and manage money like a long-haul leader is to create scalable business models. A great example of this is Convertkit, recently renamed Kit, founded in 2013 when Nathan Barry realized he needed a better way to reach his online audience so that he could sell his courses and books through email.

Nathan developed his own email marketing system, since he wasn't happy with any of the other tools out there. When he did this, he realized he had an opportunity. He could keep selling his information products to a small but faithful audience, or he could put all his cards on the table and go for broke.

Nathan kept hearing from friends and peers that he had something powerful—a software tool he could scale—but to go all in was a risk. He invested $50,000 of his own retirement to scale Convertkit, and it paid off big time. Fast-forward all these years, and the company now generates over $35 million a year in recurring revenue. To get there, Nathan had to step away from the day-to-day of writing books and instead focus on creating something bigger. He needed the right team and processes in place, and this took years to build. Now the results speak for themselves. Scale makes everything better.

If you don't have any scalable products or services, you are playing the game of business with one hand tied behind your back. You are putting yourself in a tough spot if you ever want to take a break or step away from your work to do something else. Scale allows you to invest an hour of your time and continue making money off that hour every day for the rest of your life.

When you build enough scalable products and services, you create financial independence for yourself. For example, with our Youpreneur community, Accelerator, and other products, I have thousands of paying customers receiving the same level of value as others, because 99.9 percent of those offerings are digital. When I *do* provide live coaching sessions, these happen a few times per year and always follow a "one-to-many" format, where I am coaching large groups of business owners at the same time.

This is a scalable offering, even though it takes some of my time, because whether it's 50 or 50,000 customers, I'm doing the exact same amount of work, no matter what. *That* is a business that scales. The investment you make never changes, but the potential revenue increases dramatically. When thinking about scalability, consider the following:

+ Is the model replicable?
+ Do you have the right tech and infrastructure in place to grow this thing?
+ Is there sufficient market demand for it?
+ Can your team handle exponential growth?
+ Do you have access to the required resources and capital to scale?

These are necessary questions to ask before deciding if you can, or even should, scale a business. But if you ever want to be free from having to put more hours into the machine to make more money, you should start thinking about this now.

In contrast to some of my more scalable offerings, I also enjoy running my Round Table Mastermind, which is not a scalable business. Nonetheless, I love working with this small group of high-end clients. I know that I can't grow this group to 150, 250, or 500 clients, because it just wouldn't work. I couldn't manage that kind of growth, because so much of the value I offer to this group is through one-on-one mentoring.

Not everything necessarily has to scale, so long as you have a reason for why you're doing what you're doing.

Nathan Barry wanted to grow a company that was bigger than him, and he was willing to take the needed risks to get there. He knew what he wanted, what he was willing to give up to get it, and what his nonnegotiables were. The same is true for me and my ventures. As I shared earlier, my Mastermind members have access to me via WhatsApp on certain days and at certain times. I know I've hit the maximum number of people I can serve well with this level of time commitment, so I won't negotiate on that—it's too important to me. To try to scale that would undermine the purpose of the group and feel like a compromise of integrity.

But I still look for opportunities to scale other aspects of my work. Scalability is essential to staying in business for the long haul. When everything is said and done, the subject of money will always be personal, so what you do is up to you. Still, if you want to free yourself from the constant grind of trading hours for dollars, being strategic in your approach to growth will pay huge dividends in the future. Scale what you can. It makes all the difference.

THE VALUE OF SAVING

It's great to make a lot of money, but if you keep augmenting your lifestyle every time your income goes up, you will never get ahead. As I've personally gotten more comfortable over the years, I haven't increased my spending too much. Just because I'm making more doesn't mean I have to spend more, and that's true for all of us.

Cutting costs is key. If you're always chasing the next "toy"—whether that's a boat, a watch, or a beach house—how can you adequately plan for the future? Again, it's okay to enjoy things, but as you make more, you should be saving more, not less.

Personally, I don't love spending money on things unless there is long-term value to the purchase. Given the choice between something of low quality that doesn't cost much and splurging on an item I can hand down to my kids, when I can afford to choose the latter, I do. An example of this would be the wingback leather chair I recently had custom-made after arriving back in the United Kingdom.

I wanted a nice chair placed next to our three-hundred-year-old fireplace so that I could sit and enjoy a glass of fine single malt on those damp English evenings. The chair cost a pretty penny, and delivery took eight weeks, but it'll last for generations, unlike a cheaply made one I could have picked up easily at IKEA. For me, it's not about spending a little or a lot on things but investing my hard-earned money in items that matter to me and will last a long time—or create a lot of memories.

Another area of focus for me, when it comes to setting aside money, is making sure I have all the right paperwork and systems in place. Because leaving something for my family after I'm gone is a personal goal, I've set up trusts and updated my will. I've also hired tax advisers, accountants, bookkeepers, and financial planners. One day I will not be making as much money as I am today, but I want to continue living well into my old age and providing for my family. I also want to have the means to buy an occasional trinket for myself or splurge on a fun memory-making trip with a friend.

A lot of leaders are intimidated by the idea of planning for the future. It feels out of reach—maybe even impossible—when you're just trying to get through another week, reach the end of the month, or finish the quarter. But hustle culture keeps us in a short-term grind that eventually grinds us down. Our bias for instant gratification takes more than it gives and will eventually cost a lot. If you want to be in a position where you have money to *use* instead of worrying about if you'll have enough, then a long-term, sustainable mindset toward wealth is a full-blown requirement.

CHAPTER 9

Don't Forget to Do What You Love

Long-haul leaders make time for hobbies
and activities outside work.

When I was very young, I used to regularly go to my dad's architecture office in the city. I always noticed a couple of things about that office. First, the moment you walked through the door, you were hit by the strong aroma of freshly brewed coffee. To this day, the smell of fresh coffee reminds me of my dad.

The second thing I remember vividly is the sight of all the old-school drawing tables staggered throughout the office.

This was before computer-aided design, so these tables had a weighted ruler running along one side. The weight allowed the ruler to be moved up and down, while also holding papers and drawings in place when needed.

Thick, short STABILO highlighters and fine-tipped rOtring pens were scattered all over the place. It felt like a room full of possibilities, a room of real power where the visions in my dad's and his colleagues' minds would come to life and could be seen reflected in the city skyline just outside the windows.

That was where the love of drawing began for me.

Because my father was an architect, we would draw a lot of buildings together: offices, railway stations, houses, whatever we could see. It was a wonderful way for us to bond, to spend valuable time together without having to say much.

But as I got older and became busy with my own life—starting a career, getting married, raising children—this special time with my dad dwindled and eventually stopped altogether.

And then, in 2020, when the pandemic hit, the whole country shut down. We could hardly leave our homes, and desperate to experience the city again, I decided to draw it for myself.

One of the first things I sketched was the Eiffel Tower, just from a reference photo online. Then I did another, and then another, and another, and my old passion was reignited. My dad passed away twenty years ago, but here I was, reliving those moments with him as a grown man, with my own children around me, drawing alongside me.

It was special.

Once lockdown was lifted, and we could go out and about again, I bought a sketchbook. I would go to pubs and hotels as I began traveling again, sketching on location.

There's a big difference between drawing something you're standing in front of and doing it at home with all your supplies. When you're on location, you have to sketch loosely. It's not about getting the details exactly right; it's about *suggesting* certain details. At home, you work to fill in those details, but you also have the freedom to use your imagination to make the drawing even more magical and meaningful than its real-life inspiration.

Something about the repetition and reflection required in urban sketching appeals to me. Because the initial sketch is just a suggestion, you have to come back to it, to really consider it, over and over again until you've created something new. It's much more satisfying than just taking a quick photo of a building, which you'll never look at again and probably means very little to you. But you will look back at a sketch you've created of something you admired.

Urban sketching is just one of the hobbies I value and now prioritize in my life. Yes, it's a way for me to feel close to my dad again—but it's also become a necessary lifeline to help me manage stress, find creative solutions to the problems I'm facing, and develop new skills.

The long-haul leaders I know and admire are also multifaceted people, with wide-ranging interests and surprising hobbies that appear, on the surface, to be completely unrelated to the work they do. And yet, these people are the first to tell you that the activities they do "for fun" are vital to their longevity in business, in relationships, and in life. Which makes it even more tragic that so many of us leave behind our hobbies.

WHY HOBBIES ARE THE FIRST TO GO

We all feel the squeeze of life from time to time. We're working on deadlines, we've got loads to do at home, and we just can't seem to find the time for something that feels *fun*. Over 50 percent of leaders and entrepreneurs in my network told me that they occasionally, rarely, or *never* have time to pursue hobbies or activities "just for fun."

Time constraints are the primary reason most people tend to give up their beloved hobbies from childhood and early adulthood. This is especially true for entrepreneurs. Granted, running a business *is* time-consuming. A lot of leaders find themselves juggling responsibilities with family and managing their businesses all at the same time. Having to tend to so many different priorities at the same time doesn't leave much room for anything extra.

But I think we lose a lot when we lose our hobbies.

In the last chapter, we talked about the relentless pursuit of more—particularly money—which tends to haunt a lot of business leaders. When I ask clients why they've given up passions they used to have, one of the top reasons they share, after time, is money. Since hobbies don't typically make us money (although they can!) and sometimes even cost some money, many people tend to view them as a distraction from the work they're supposed to be doing.

The other reason people quit their passions is FOMO (fear of missing out). Leadership is incredibly competitive, and the impression we entrepreneurs sometimes give is that everything is a zero-sum game. If you're not working at 1,000 percent, then you're *losing*. Or so the thinking goes.

I see many of my clients spend a lot of time obsessing over their competition, comparing themselves to others without realizing how different they often are from their competitors. If you're really competitive and you've got a fear of missing out, then you might see snipping away at a bonsai tree or sketching a cool new office building as time that could be better spent. Like coming up with a new marketing strategy, for example. Or you could be spending that same time attending an industry event or closing the next deal. The options are endless.

There's nothing wrong with feeling competitive and motivated to work hard, but it can become unhealthy when work starts to replace all the things we do for fun. Unfortunately, most clients don't even realize that losing their hobbies is the first sign that their focus is on the wrong priorities.

There's also the impression that hobbies are childish or silly. While it's normal for kids to be involved in all kinds of activities, it's not something adults do as much. It's almost like we feel guilty doing something so carefree and life affirming.

This has to stop. We need to reconnect with the activities that bring us joy, or we're in bigger trouble than we realize. We need to make room for the things we can do without judgment, without trying to meet all our key performance indicators, and without worrying about a strategic plan or goal. The more time I've devoted to hobbies in the last few years, the more I've realized how essential they are for my mental health and productivity. In short, the better I play, the better I work.

HOBBIES PROTECT YOUR MENTAL HEALTH

Many of history's highest performers were hobbyists.

In the wee hours of the morning, you might expect to find retired soccer (or, as we in the United Kingdom like to say, "football") superstar David Beckham resting after a long day. But you might be surprised to discover that he's often up early building LEGO sets, a hobby that his wife teases him about.

Winston Churchill had a surprising obsession, as well, that occupied much of his time when he wasn't out winning wars, leading a country, or negotiating with political opponents. He was a dedicated painter. Although he was modest about his achievements as an artist, his works were quite good and received high praise. Churchill attacked the canvas with the same passion and determination that he did everything else in his life.

Long-haul leaders often find that their hobbies are indispensable. Engaging in a hobby gives us the opportunity to unwind, relax, and recharge. Many hobbies require just enough effort to put us in an amazing mental state of *flow*, where everything else seems to melt away. We forget the pressures and stresses of the outside world and become completely absorbed in the activity right in front of us. It's like a form of meditation.

When we're pursuing activities and hobbies that we really enjoy, we also tend to feel more positive and hopeful for the future. When I come back from a weekend of hiking, family time, and tending to my bonsais, I'm always ready to rock and roll, invigorated with a renewed sense of focus and energy. The effects are remarkable.

And it's no wonder, since studies have shown that the flow state experienced when listening to music, sketching, or interacting with other forms of art creates alpha brain waves, which are associated with deep relaxation and rest. Pursuing hobbies may be literally healing for us, protecting us from the harmful effects of stress.

That certainly seems to be the case for my friend Mike Morrison.

Mike is the founder of Membership Geeks, a community of leaders who run online membership programs, and Membership Academy, a training platform that helps leaders build their own communities around the things they love. In fact, Mike helped me build the Youpreneur community and membership program years ago.

In 2017, Mike came to share his knowledge as a speaker at the inaugural Youpreneur Summit in London, and I handed out London-themed LEGO sets to all the presenters that year. You could build the London Eye, Trafalgar Square, Big Ben, and other iconic landmarks. It was the perfect way for me to honor my hometown and my love of LEGO, but I had no idea it would be life changing for Mike, who told me,

I must have been six years old. I'd gotten my first and only LEGO set for Christmas, which my dad and his best friend built for me on Boxing Day because I was too young to build it. But it was mine. It was this cool little police station. And my friend came over after Christmas, and about five minutes into being there, he knocked it off the shelf and it smashed onto the floor. For years, I had this half-demolished police station just sitting there in a pile of bricks, and I wasn't able to patch it all back together.

So then, this [new set] was the first LEGO set I'd really had [since childhood]. And it was fun . . . uniquely distracting. It was something I could just completely turn my attention to, without picking up my phone every few minutes or getting distracted by TV. LEGO is just really soothing and calming and therapeutic. And it's kind of fun to have this cool-looking thing afterwards. So I bought another set and another set.

Mike knows the struggles of being a business owner and how all-consuming it can be. "When you enjoy running your business," he said, "and even in those times when you don't, you're not logging out at 5 p.m. You're always thinking; your brain is on it. And it's difficult to find something that takes you out of that completely, that closes down even that little part of your brain that's always on alert for what's happening in the business."

Mike has been through phases in his career where he pushed himself too hard, working eighteen-hour days and operating on very little sleep and a lot of caffeine. He's burned out before and suffered from mental health challenges in his twenties. His business suffered for it, and residual anxieties still come up on occasion.

Being an entrepreneur can be stressful, and as Mike says, "You need to give yourself that mental vacation from what you're doing."

Today, Mike has elaborate LEGO sets in every room of his house. He even hosts a podcast dedicated to discussing the most exciting LEGO builds. This "new" hobby has helped him stay grounded and not get lost in the pressures of work. No surprise, he now runs his seven-figure business very successfully—and at a fantastic profit margin.

Who knew that having fun could be so productive?

EXERCISE ISN'T ENOUGH

When I ask my clients what their hobbies are, many of them say exercise. And there's no doubt that exercise has been proven to relieve stress and improve mental well-being. Leaders in my audience listed a number of physical activities that help them to de-stress:

- Walking
- Swimming
- Cycling
- Working out at the gym
- Playing tennis
- Doing CrossFit and Pilates

All of these activities are good and worthwhile. Exercise is absolutely necessary for both our physical and mental health. But I don't see exercise as a hobby or a pastime. I see it as a nonnegotiable.

We know that if we exercise, we will live a healthier and longer life. It's like saying eating is a hobby. Sure, most of us probably enjoy eating, but it doesn't quite count as a hobby if it's something that's essential to your health.

Hobbies, ideally, go beyond the things required for mere survival. Hobbies are activities we engage in for pleasure, personal learning, and skill building. They are aligned with our personal passions, things we find intensely interesting, activities that we are curious about.

This isn't to say that hobbies can't or shouldn't be physically demanding or give us a good workout. Of course, they can—but the intention behind them matters. Going out for a run because you know you need to lose weight is not a hobby. On the other hand, joining a Latin dancing class because you're interested in the culture and want to learn the complicated steps so you can dance the salsa like they do on *Dancing with the Stars*—that's a hobby.

And it just might be the push you need to help you achieve a breakthrough.

HOBBIES HELP US BREAK THROUGH

Personal views and opinions aside, most of us know of Elon Musk. He's started several businesses in a wide variety of seemingly unrelated fields: aerospace, cars, personal finance, neuroscience, artificial intelligence—even underground tunneling. Most of us spend our lives cultivating just one or two areas of expertise, things we become known for in our fields. We create a unified "brand" and stick with it, for better or worse. But not Elon.

What sets Musk apart from other leaders is that he's a voracious learner. As a child, he read up to two books a day across a variety of genres, including science fiction, philosophy, computer science, biography, and more. He was always thirsty to learn, a habit that continued into adulthood.

It's easy to look at the elements that make up the serial entrepreneur as different, but I think they're more connected than that. As a voracious reader, Elon Musk is taking the concepts and skills he's learned in one context (say, engineering) and applying them to a completely different context (like neuroscience). He is an expert not just in one discipline but in blending disciplines to solve complicated problems.

So far, this skill has helped him create the world's most effective and efficient electric vehicle and launch rockets into space. Not bad, if you ask me. Of course, not everything Elon tries works. But he has enough practice plugging new solutions into old problems that he's often able to see past assumptions others might make and approach an old field with fresh eyes. And I think a lot of that comes from his early fascination with reading so many different types of books.

I've come to believe that having a hobby is one of the superpowers long-haul leaders use to solve complex problems. Many hobbies, like playing chess, have an obvious benefit in improving critical thinking and planning several moves ahead. But even hobbies like gardening or language learning can help us practice patience in working out tricky situations.

HOBBIES BOOST OUR CONFIDENCE

When I first started learning about bonsai, I was most worried about killing the trees. I desperately didn't want to do that. So I had to go down a little bit of a rabbit hole to find out how trees work, how their roots gather and provide nutrients from the soil, and how the foliage uses photosynthesis to convert sunlight into glucose for growth.

I was interested in creating nice-looking trees, but that outcome became the secondary focus. The biggest thing was understanding how the trees worked and how my actions might affect them. Thankfully, I found a bonsai artist who tutored me for a few days to help me learn to prune branches, wire the tree and position branches, and not only avoid killing the trees but ultimately create that nice aesthetic.

Now I have a lovely garden to spend time in, but I also have the pride of knowing I've cultivated a new skill and accomplished something worthwhile with my own hands.

Learning to do something new boosts our confidence and self-efficacy. We have the evidence in front of us, whether in the form of a beautiful bonsai or an intricate watercolor painting, that we can do hard things. I've found that when everything else in your life might seem to be going downhill or you feel like you're failing again and again, seeing success in a meaningful hobby can give you the lift you need to stay strong in the face of challenges.

HOBBIES BRING US TOGETHER

I've mentioned my mate Pat Flynn before. He's a great YouTuber and podcaster, a coach for many leaders. But what you may not know is that Pat Flynn is obsessed with Pokémon.

It all started when he and his family were visiting us here in the United Kingdom. We got to talking about Pokémon one morning, as my son Charlie and I would often buy packs of the cards and open them together.

Pat and I started watching YouTube videos of other creators opening packs. And that afternoon we went out and purchased a whole bunch of packs and opened them up with our kids before dinner. We had a lot of fun and many laughs, and a new memory was created for our families.

This is where I thought that memory ended.

Always open to opportunities, however, Pat saw that a lot of the YouTubers had good Pokémon knowledge but didn't know a lot about running a YouTube channel—something my friend is excellent at. So he started his own Pokémon channel, called Deep Pocket Monster, where he documents his journey to collect Pokémon cards with his kids.

The channel has been incredibly successful. In less than a year, he had 100,000 subscribers. And in just over two years, it's reached over 750,000 subscribers. By the time this book is published, I have no doubt he'll have hit the 1 million subscriber mark.

But the subscribers aren't what make the channel worth it for him. For Pat, Pokémon will always be about connecting with families that enjoy the same passion for the hobby. His authenticity and the fun he has with his viewers keeps drawing people in.

Similarly, I know that my hobbies make me a better person, mostly a better father, which is the most important role in my life. When my children see me enjoying hobbies, developing new skills, and creating works of art, they are inspired as well. My youngest, Cassie, calls herself the "nature girl." She likes to go out on walks with me on our property while I'm sketching in my nature journal. My son Charlie similarly enjoys sitting with me when I'm working on my bonsai trees. When they see me drawing and painting, wiring and pruning, they want to join in as well. These kids already love art and nature.

I know that I'm teaching them to respect and admire wildlife. They're learning how to have patience and be intentional with every action. This is time without cell phones, disconnected from devices and the noise of the online world. We're all getting vitamin D and soaking in the calming sounds and scenes of our home. Best of all, we're creating core memories together that we'll all treasure for the rest of our lives.

Talking about my hobbies helps me to be a more influential leader for my clients and the people who follow my work from afar. My audience knows that I'm not all about work, work, work all the time. I talk about my experiences with burnout and the fact that I won't let it happen again, which is important. But I also show them what I'm doing to make sure it doesn't happen again. I love sharing my passions and hobbies with clients because it opens the door to learning what other interests we may share.

Now I'll often have clients ask after my bonsai or ask to see one of my sketches. And I do the same with them. I love seeing the accomplishments of my Mastermind members and encouraging them to pursue their passions.

WHAT WILL YOU REMEMBER?

Our hobbies—the things we do purely for enjoyment and rest—have a tremendous impact on who we are as leaders and how we show up for our teams.

When life gets a little tough, it's easy to become consumed by those challenges and lose sight of who you are and what you're all about. By staying committed to our hobbies, even in the midst of life's challenges, we reaffirm how important they are in our lives. Hobbies remind us of the things that bring us joy, in the times when we need it most.

If you're struggling to think of hobbies that might be fun for you to pursue, ask yourself the following questions to spark a few ideas:

- What activities or interests bring you joy or relaxation outside your work responsibilities?
- Is there a skill or hobby you enjoyed as a child or teenager that you've set aside over the years?
- What do you find yourself naturally curious about or wanting to learn more about in your free time?
- Do you have a creative side that you haven't fully explored yet? What artistic or creative activities appeal to you?

As I begin to look back at my life thus far, I find that although I'm proud of my work and career achievements, it's the quality time I've spent with the people I love, doing the things that I love, that I remember the most.

What will *you* remember?

CHAPTER 10

Build a Legacy

Long-haul leaders leave a lasting impact.

Nelson Mandela. Aretha Franklin. Albert Einstein. Bruce Lee. Margaret Thatcher. Kobe Bryant.

What did these people have in common? They were clearly masters of their craft, individuals whose names we still remember for their greatness. Some lived longer lives than others, and some spent a surprisingly short time on earth. But all of them, in their own way, were long-haul leaders.

Now these people were no strangers to hard work. They even had their seasons of hustle. But to truly accomplish greatness, you can't just sprint through life. You have to leave a legacy, and that takes intention.

These people pushed themselves to the max and persisted in spite of incredible odds against them. They set goals and achieved their vision. They went against the grain, defying others' expectations of them, and achieved something we still marvel at today.

So, how did they do it? How did they have such an impact? It wasn't an accident.

The great ones from history knew the importance of pacing themselves, of having a vision for the change they wanted to make. They also knew such an impact was bigger than any single person. They knew what it meant to do impactful work, to live a life where people don't just remember what you did but what you did it for.

Think of some of the people you admire, those who lived incredible lives that you would love to emulate. These individuals probably didn't just do one thing that they are still remembered for. More than likely, you admire their persistence, their vision, their skill. And in all likelihood, the greatness they achieved wasn't due to a single event or cause. Rather, it was the accumulation of many moments over the course of an entire lifetime. This is what makes a legend. This is what creates a legacy.

In this chapter, I want to introduce you to leaders who are working hard, in sustainable ways, to create the impact they want to leave. I also want to share with you what legacy is and why each of us is creating one now, whether we realize it or not.

Most of all, though, I want you to remember that if you spend your whole life hustling, you will never have the time or energy to build a real legacy. You'll be remembered for your hard work, sure, but nothing else. Because a hustler can never take their eye off the ball, they are never able to step back and get a wider perspective. Creating a legacy takes intention and time, so we need to get started now.

WHO, NOT WHAT

Most of us spend a good part of life accumulating things. Money, awards, clothes, collectibles, even domain names (one I am especially guilty of)! We're taught to do this from childhood, watching our parents do the same. But we often forget that we don't get to take any of this stuff with us—not a single thing! So, at some point, we have to start thinking not about getting more but about letting go.

Imagine, for example, a beach. The tide comes in, the tide goes out. You can't control it, but you know the water will come, and the water will go—and there's nothing you can do to change it. This is a lot like how life works. Nothing lasts forever, not even our most significant accomplishments or accolades. Success may come, and success may go. We will always want to hold onto any good thing for as long as we can, but it will eventually end. After a while, even *we* won't be here to enjoy what we've accomplished. Life is all a training ground for learning to let go.

Your legacy planning begins today. If you don't plan ahead while the "tide" is in and you have the opportunity to make an impact on others, then when it's all done, all that will be left is a pile of sand. Lots of people say they want to leave a legacy, but the operative word here is "leave." If we spend most of our time focused on us, on what we can achieve and accumulate, there won't be much to leave for anyone else. The impact we want to make requires that at some point we learn to step outside ourselves and consider the bigger picture.

We'll talk in a moment about the things you can leave behind (as well as what you can't), but the first thing I want you to understand is that legacy is about people. That's what matters most—not *what* you're leaving behind but *whom* you're leaving it to.

When you think about the people who will inherit your legacy, you probably think first about loved ones. I do. Family always comes first. But as leaders, you and I have the potential to leave an impact that extends beyond family. We get to leave something, if we plan for it, to our team members, our clients and customers, our friends, and maybe even our community or more.

Thanks to the power of social media and the internet, all of us have a broader reach than most previous generations in history. We need to act like it. Legacy is defined by the work we do, the life we lead, and the people we impact. When you're hustling, it's hard to think about legacy, much less plan for it.

Because, when you get down to it, hustle is about you: what *you* can do, how fast *you* can do it, and what *you* will accomplish. Legacy, on the other hand, is about empowering others. The focus shifts from you to *them*.

So whom do you want to benefit from your legacy? Spend some time brainstorming these people. Make a list. Then consider what you want to leave each of them.

When I think about my family, for example, I'm focused on financial security and education. Ensuring my family is safe and has access to the absolute best education and opportunities is paramount. I also place an emphasis on passing on family traditions (such as our annual sabbatical) and sharing old stories. I want the story and traditions of the Ducker clan to continue.

I also try to lead by example. Our family values matter a lot to me. I want my sons to know the importance of being a gentleman and providing for their families. I want my children to know the importance of providing for their families, and also to know what it means to be loved and adored. I want to give my kids the confidence to chase down their dreams, no matter what.

A lot of leaders think about these things too late in life. You may have accomplished a lot through your work, but if you aren't sharing the keys to your success with others, then what chance do you have of passing on what you've learned? Our work ethic, how we treat people, even our resilience as leaders will always serve as a powerful model for others, especially family. This is one of those intangible legacies that's hard to measure but shows over time.

For my friends, I consider what values and lessons I want to impart. This includes the importance of integrity in business, perseverance in pursuit of any meaningful goal, and generosity toward others. I do my best to share these values both through my actions and in my words. I want my friends to know what I'm about, what I think truly matters, and I hope some of those lessons rub off on them. I also want to be remembered as someone who supported his friends' growth, as well as their plans for the future—and of course, I want to have lots of memorable experiences with these people.

When it comes to work, I want to leave a legacy for my colleagues and employees, to have had a positive impact on the people I worked with. I want my clients and customers to know how much I cared about them and their success—I want them to know I was always cheering them on. And lastly, I want to see the impact of our work with charitable organizations and to know that the impact will continue long after I'm gone.

For me, this is all about people. It starts and ends with relationships.

START WITH YOU

The first way to leave a legacy is through your example. I know one of the values I want to leave to my team is lifelong learning. We've got to continue to learn in order to continue to lead. I demonstrate this to the people I lead by always reading a new book and talking about it, exploring new ideas, and surrounding myself with others who challenge me.

The other way we can create a legacy is by how we invest our time and energy in others. If we're not consistently investing in ourselves, our teams, our clients, and our systems, then we won't have built anything that will last. I want to continue providing value, showing up for my clients, and being a rock for the people I come in contact with.

When I am at a conference speaking, or if I meet someone at a dinner party after a workshop, I hope they come up to me and talk about what it meant for them. I want to know when they discovered my work and how it's helped them develop their business and their life. I want to leave a legacy based on other people taking action, realizing their dreams, and providing a great life for themselves and their families.

Like my friend Carrie Wilkerson, author of *The Barefoot Executive* and another long-haul leader who's cultivating a legacy based on excellence and value for her clients.

Carrie has worked with some of the biggest names in personal productivity and leadership. I love that her focus on getting results for her clients has never wavered. She's got a tough-love mentality that motivates her clients far beyond what they could accomplish themselves. But she also knows when to stop working and focus on her family and her personal life.

Carrie is creating her legacy every day by living out her values in front of others. I know I have personally benefited from seeing not only what she's done but what she's chosen *not* to do. Actions speak louder than words, but sometimes the most significant action is the decision *not* to do something.

Carrie has mastered the art of saying no to almost everything other than what aligns with her purpose. She's tuned into her own LifeOS and lets her intentions guide her.

Another legacy-minded leader is my good friend Amy Porterfield. Amy got her start working with world-renowned performance coach Tony Robbins but ended up branching out on her own to eventually build a huge media empire. Today she's an eight-figure business owner who helps people all around the world achieve their own dreams of launching successful businesses. Through her podcast, social media channels, events, and online courses, she is making a huge impact on others—but she started with herself.

She has always made an example of herself in her health, her work habits, and even her relationships, sharing her values every step of the way. When she eventually retires or steps down from leading her company, Amy will know with full confidence that she's left a huge mark on others. She will be able to look back at the tens of thousands of businesses and entrepreneurs who can trace their success back to her. She started by focusing on improving her own life, then sharing what she learned with others and helping them succeed as well.

The work we do has a ripple effect in ways we cannot fully understand now. If you have influence, even over just a handful of people, do not take this for granted. Your impact matters, more than you realize, and you have an opportunity to make the most of it every single day. Set an example with your actions and be intentional about this. How you show up each and every day is part of the legacy you leave.

Remember that one of the key areas in the LifeOS is meaningful work. Legacy isn't just about heirloom timepieces and family traditions; it's about the people you work with, lead, and serve professionally on a daily basis.

WHEN IT'S NO LONGER ABOUT YOU

Prioritizing legacy now is about more than what you leave behind when you leave this life. It's also about more than just the impact you have on clients and customers. It also includes your colleagues: the people you work with and how you influence them on a daily basis. You won't, after all, be in a position of leadership forever, so plan for that end now. Be ready to make your transition before it happens, while you still have a choice.

Long-haul leaders never lose sight of the fact that their leadership is temporary. This opportunity to lead won't last forever, whether you decide to retire and move on from your current role or the decision is made for you. These leaders think intentionally about the next generation of leaders while they're still in charge. And you should do the same.

This is where my chief operating officer (and daughter), Chloe, comes into play. I hope the Youpreneur community continues long after I decide to hang up my hat as CEO of the company. We have trained thousands of people in how to build a strong personal brand business, and the work we've done isn't going to disappear, even when I'm no longer leading the company.

We've still got all our digital content, our live-event recordings, the book, the podcast, and so much more. I've been the caretaker of all that work for a long time, but it's Chloe's turn to grab hold of the baton and move the company into the next stage of growth.

My friend Michael Hyatt has done the same. Michael built an incredibly successful business based around his expertise, his personality, and his personal brand. But then, slowly but surely, he transitioned it into a new business, so that Michael Hyatt & Co. became Full Focus.

The community Michael built is no longer based on him. It's based on the ideas that he and his team have developed together for over a decade. "At some point," he wrote about the decision to rebrand the company and expand its reach beyond his own name, "I crossed the line where *it was no longer about me. It was about us.*"

He too has placed one of his daughters, Megan Hyatt Miller, at the helm, running the company day to day while Michael continues to be involved. He is a great example of how you can transition from having a personal brand to building a legacy around a vision that is bigger than any single person, passing that baton to the next generation while personally stepping back from the spotlight.

When it comes to the legacy you want to leave, I challenge you to consider the concrete ways you've invested in other people's lives. Think about the opportunities you still have to do this. Because at the end of the day, a leader's job is to grow other people. Everything else is just gravy.

Some of the leaders I look up to are Richard Branson, Jeff Bezos, and Steve Jobs. Although sometimes controversial figures, these men have had an impact far greater than most of us ever will. You cannot discount their legacies. Just look at Virgin, Amazon, and Apple. Think about how many people these companies employ and how many customers they serve. Without a doubt, they've changed the way all of us live.

Sometimes being a leader means making hard calls that not everyone will understand or agree with. But it goes beyond pleasing yourself or others. Real leadership is about asking, "What is best for *us*?" What is best for the company, the movement you are a part of, the vision that you have for the future? And how can you share that with others who can carry the torch long after you're gone? That's what my heroes have done and a large part of the legacy I want to leave my team and my family.

The legacy we leave at work is often a gift to the world, something that may change lives for years. The people who benefit from our legacy may never know *us* personally. And that's okay. That's why the most meaningful legacy you leave has nothing to do with you. It's not about being remembered. It's about giving back, investing in others, and helping raise up leaders like yourself.

WHAT WE REALLY LEAVE BEHIND

When most people think about legacy, they tend to think about stuff. They might talk about their wills, any property they own, charitable contributions they want to make, or maybe even some cash or investments they're holding onto. They might think about the family wedding ring or grandpa's old war medal.

Personally, I think about my two sons wearing my Rolexes and clipping my bonsai trees. I think about my eldest daughter flipping through the pages of her grandmother's prayer book, which I still keep in my desk drawer. I think about my youngest daughter peeking through my binoculars while out on a nature walk, thinking about how she used to do this with Daddy.

There's nothing wrong with having some things to share with your family and friends. But that's not all there is. Really, the stuff we leave behind should represent the memories embedded in those things. That's where the real legacy lies, in the intangible lessons and values we leave.

Many of us had to work hard to get where we are in life, and we want our loved ones to understand the lessons that took us years to learn so they don't have to repeat our same mistakes. We want our children to remember what matters most, what we taught them about life. My dad left a legacy for me of hard work, teaching me to always do my best, to have integrity in everything I say and do, and to take good care of my family. I know he would be proud not just of what I've accomplished but of who I've become. I want to know that when I'm gone, part of who I am will be passed down to my kids too.

My children and I have already had plenty of conversations around these topics, talking about respect, admiration, and supportiveness. I've tried to teach them what I believe, passing on my values to them and sharing my mistakes. We've talked about saving money, being a good friend, and having faith in something bigger than you. These are simple lessons, but they matter to me and represent a life well lived.

Everyone has a tangible legacy—the financial and material gifts we leave behind—and these things can be useful. But they're also limited. Every human life, however, has a whole treasure trove of lessons, mistakes, and values to be shared. There's no limit to this intangible legacy we get to leave behind. We just have to be intentional about it.

The ideas you share with your kids can ripple down for generations. The impact you make with your kindness or generosity can continue for centuries. These immaterial offerings go a lot farther than cash ever could, and we need to remember this. Some people spend their whole lives thinking about the stuff they're going to leave behind when what matters most is not stuff at all. It's a memory, a conversation, a lesson. This is what people will remember most about you. This is your real legacy.

What we leave behind goes beyond people remembering us. Because eventually, even our names will be forgotten. But the impact we made, the mark we left on the lives of others, can go on, if not forever, then for a very long time. So let's look, practically, at how we can begin planning for this impact.

There's no doubt in my mind that the best way to leave a legacy is by working hard every day to become the best version of yourself. Don't wait for some distant time in the future when you'll be more generous, patient, or understanding. Don't assume you'll always have more time to call that friend or show up to support someone you care about. Don't think that going to the gym or creating a better nighttime routine will always be available to you. It won't. If you see an opportunity to be the kind of person you want to be, don't wait another minute. Do it now.

Similarly, you can't keep waiting for more time to invest in the things you love. If you don't take the time to use your skills—even the skills you've developed in pursuit of something fun like urban sketching, gardening, playing an instrument, or collecting Pokémon cards—you will lose those skills.

Think about the life you would want to live if time weren't an issue. Although retirement is something many of us look forward to, it's also one of the hardest transitions most of us will make—especially for entrepreneurs and people who have been investing so much of themselves into their careers for the majority of their lives.

I believe everyone should start training for retirement *now*. Not only will you reap the benefits of more rest, relaxation, and enjoyment in the midst of your current career, but you'll be setting yourself up for an easier transition into the next season of life, whenever it comes.

Lastly, when it comes to leaving a personal legacy, remember to look at the closest people in your life—your spouse, your kids, your best friends. What do they need from you? How do you want them to remember who you were? What memories can you make with them today, this week, this month? Building a legacy starts now. Don't wait another day.

As an example, if my children ever need me for something, they get my attention. No matter what's happening, no matter where we are, I am always available—either in person or on the phone. When everything is said and done, they will know that, for sure.

Special days out with my family, both as a whole and with individual members, are important to me too. Like going to the British Grand Prix with my eldest, CJ; or a princess experience party with my youngest, Cassandra; or a couples yoga retreat with my wife, Erz.

IT'S UP TO YOU

In March 2024, longtime entrepreneur Alex Charfen made a surprising announcement to his thousands of fans and followers. After decades of coaching entrepreneurs and raising up leaders, he and his wife, Cadey, were shutting everything down. In a final series of podcast episodes, he explained the thinking behind the decision:

> Cadey and I have worked the last twenty years to build resources, to become independently wealthy, to have no debt, and to have really strong investments that can support us for a long time. And in the last few months, we've been talking about our

business—what we're doing and what we want to do. And for the first time in twenty years, both of us have aligned around the decision that there's something bigger for us, that there's something more important for us, that there's something more exciting for us. We don't know what it is, but we have some ideas.

Alex and Cadey are barely fifty years old. They have a lot of time left to do the things they love, and they know it. It's not uncommon for someone in their season of life to double down on what they've done and keep hustling harder in search of something bigger or better. But they have decided that what they've done, and what they have, is enough right now.

Now, before it's too late, they're considering what they'll leave behind, not just for their kids but for the communities they care about. They're entering a season of quiet and rest so that they can discern how they want to live the rest of their lives to create the most meaningful impact.

I asked Alex how he thinks about his legacy now versus what he thought when he first became an entrepreneur. "I used to just want to make money," he told me. "I remember wanting to make $100,000 in a year, and I did it, and I didn't even know. And then I wanted to make a million dollars in a year, and I knew when I did that. Then I wanted to make a million dollars in a month, then a million dollars in a day. I've done all those things. But the money gets to a point where it's not as important as the number of people you've helped and what type of impact you make."

Alex and Cadey could keep on making money. That is certainly a choice that would leave a financial legacy to the people and causes they care about. And they may do just that. But they don't want to just live their lives on autopilot—whatever decision they make will be thoroughly thought through and based on the values they care most about.

I know what you're thinking. *Must be nice.* I mean, if you were making a million dollars a day, it wouldn't be that hard to quit working and focus on something else—*would* it?

At times, leaving a legacy can seem like a luxury. But that's why it's so important to think more about the lessons and values we want to leave rather than the money and stuff we have or don't have. The stuff is limited; it can only take you so far. That's what I take from Alex, someone who's made more money than most of us will ever dream of having. And he's saying, "Enough is enough. It's time to focus on more important issues."

In one of his final podcasts, he offered some parting advice to his audience, talking about the pitfalls of a constant hustle mentality. "The more present and grounded we are," he said, "the more intentional we are with what we build, the more we take care of ourselves, the more it allows us to see that we're moving in a direction we want. And the more that we actually integrate who we are with what we want to do—that's where we actually create massive outcomes in the world."

That's the opportunity available to each of us right now, no matter where we are in our careers, no matter how much money we've made (or not). Each of us has to decide what legacy we want to leave. And the best way to do that is to get quiet and reflect so that you can decide what impact you want to create.

WE GET TO PRACTICE

Every change in our lives, every time we walk into a new space and leave another behind, is an opportunity to think carefully about what we want to leave behind for others and whom we want to leave it to. I've already left multiple legacies, and you have too—whether you realize it or not.

Every new beginning comes from an ending, and that is always an opportunity to leave something behind for others. When my family moved from the Philippines, we left a legacy. When I quit jobs and sold companies, I left a legacy.

Whenever we experience any change in life, we are leaving something of ourselves behind. Are we being intentional? When my first two kids left the house, that was an opportunity to leave a little legacy for them, to share some advice and offer a little "old man" wisdom if they wanted to hear it.

For my eldest son, my advice was mostly focused on being smart with money and making sure he had some rainy-day funds put to one side. With my daughter, it was mostly around not settling for someone other than what she really, truly wanted in a partner.

Anytime a relationship ends or you have a health scare, anytime you meet a stranger on a plane—that's an opportunity for legacy. And as with anything, the more we practice doing it, the better we get.

Every day, you are living the legacy you will leave behind tomorrow. I've already left some legacies, and I still have more to offer.

What's yours?

CHAPTER 11

A Long-Haul Life

Long-haul leaders go the distance
in business . . . and in life.

My 2023 sabbatical was one to remember. We celebrated my fiftieth birthday with a trip to London and stayed at the Corinthia Hotel in a gorgeous suite, where my youngest, Cassie, was delighted by the fact that we had a butler. We hosted a party with fifty of my closest friends and family from all over the world on a boat once owned by Richard Branson.

A three-piece acoustic jazz trio played as we toured the River Thames, passing all the historic landmarks: the London Eye, Big Ben, London Bridge. We ate birthday cake in the shape of a bonsai tree and toasted with champagne. Erz shared a compilation video of messages from dear friends who couldn't make it in person, all wishing me a happy birthday.

It was an amazing time. But by far, the highlight of the experience was when my oldest friend, Kaveh, the only person in my life who knew my parents when they were living, stood up to make a speech: "If your mum and dad were still alive," he said, "even though they'd be hella old by now, they would be incredibly proud of everything you've achieved, especially the way you've helped others."

Later, Kaveh told me that even though he didn't know many of the other people on the boat, he enjoyed meeting everyone and could tell I keep good company. His words stuck with me. I think that is one of my proudest achievements in life, that in the last twenty years or so, I've made good friends. The relationships I've fostered and developed—seen easily on that landmark day of my life—are evidence of the work I've done to put my priorities in the right place. It's rewarding and kind of humbling, to be honest.

I've not always been primarily focused on relationships. There were times in my life, as you now know, that were all about the next buck or big thing. I always believed family and friends were important but didn't always make time for them. Had I not experienced a series of wake-up calls, I might never have made it to that birthday in the first place.

If hustling delivered me to burnout's door, nearly destroying my career and life, it was the choices I made afterward that brought me to that day, surrounded by my family and friends, appreciating and celebrating all I've been given. This is what I remind my clients. The choices we make now affect how far we will go and how well.

Life is a marathon. If you want to enjoy it, you have to make intentional decisions along the way to pace yourself, to bring light and joy to your own life, and to spend time with the people who matter most to you. You don't get this kind of community, the kind of friendship in your life where people fly halfway across the globe to celebrate you, without long-term investments.

When you live by the rules of hustle, everything is disposable. It's money in, money out. People in, people out. Time disappears before you realize it's gone, and it's too late to put first things first. But long-haul living is deeper than that. The LifeOS framework isn't a collection of random advice. It's the accumulation of all I've learned in half a century of life and what I practice on a daily basis and preach to my friends, clients, and colleagues. It may not be for everyone, but I truly believe it is the best path for me. And that day on the boat solidified that decision for me.

THE TRAITS OF A LONG-HAUL LEADER

I hope after reading this book you're convinced that hustling is a short-term game, a sprint. If you're good at it, you may be able to go fast, even far—for a while. But once you burn out, and it *will* happen if you keep going at that pace, you'll be out of the race, maybe for good.

Genghis Khan and his Mongolian hordes used to have several horses so that they could switch between them, running each horse to its limits, then moving on to the next one. This was the design of the Pony Express too. The mail carriers calculated the exact distance they could ride each horse as hard and as fast as possible, then they would switch at a station, and repeat the process, exchanging one horse for the next until they reached their destination.

The myth was that the carriers would ride their horses until they died, literally running them into the ground. But that wasn't true. The Mongolian warriors and early mail carriers knew that no animal could hustle forever. And they planned accordingly. We don't have the luxury of swapping ourselves out for a new version, though. This is the only life and body we get.

If we want to go the distance in business and in life, we have to take things at a more sustainable pace. Navigating the complexities of running a business demands a commitment to personal well-being. I also want you to enjoy the journey along the way. Leadership is a marathon. Prioritizing your health, setting boundaries, managing your time, and investing in people and activities you love are not just beneficial; they are essential. The most successful leaders are those who recognize that their well-being is linked to the health of their businesses and the people around them.

I created the following acronym as a shortcut to help my clients keep in mind the core characteristics of long-haul leaders. If you embody these qualities, you'll be able to stay focused on your purpose, committed to the intentions you set for every area of your life.

L—Learner: Long-haul leaders are committed to continuous learning and personal development, recognizing that growth is a lifelong journey.

O—Open-minded: Long-haul leaders maintain an open-minded approach, embracing new ideas and perspectives over time.

N—Nurturing: Long-haul leaders nurture the people they are surrounded by, fostering growth and development in others.

G—Grounded: Long-haul leaders remain grounded in their values and principles, even as they navigate change and uncertainty.

H—Health: Long-haul leaders prioritize their physical, mental, and emotional health, recognizing that well-being is essential for sustained success.

A—Adaptable: Long-haul leaders adapt to circumstances and embrace change as an opportunity for growth and innovation.

U—Unifying: Long-haul leaders bring people together, bridging differences and building consensus to achieve shared success.

L—Legacy: Long-haul leaders are focused on leaving a lasting legacy of positive impact in the lives of those they love and work with.

THE INVITATION TO A LONG-HAUL LIFE

I know you want to accomplish great things. So do I. Like Alex Charfen, Michael Hyatt, Joana Galvao, and the other leaders I've mentioned in this book, I have a lot left to do. I know the option to hustle will always be there. Sometimes it might be the right choice. But I'll only be able to make it if I've been wisely managing my health, finances, time, and relationships.

If I go back to pushing myself too hard, to prioritizing *more* for the sake of more, then I'll end up right back where I was before. Burnt out. Running myself into the ground.

You see, burning out is a symptom of immaturity. It is a sign of living recklessly, without discipline, limits, or boundaries. My second near-burnout experience was an invitation to live life differently. To embrace some limits and enjoy the people, work, activities, and time available to me.

To become a long-haul leader.

I hope it doesn't take the same circumstances before you'll accept your own invitation. This book isn't just an exploration of long-haul leadership. It's a challenge to make the most of your life. To create something out of the opportunities available to us. And to go the distance in your work, relationships, and personal life, so that your time on earth counts for something.

I've said it before, and I'll say it again: I am in it for the long haul. There is no other option in my mind. And I hope you are too. See you at the finish line.

THE LONG-HAUL LEADER ASSESSMENT

In order to maximize the teachings in this book, I've put together a short online assessment that focuses on the four major areas of the Long-Haul Leader LifeOS—namely, personal mastery, love and relationships, hobbies, and impactful work.

It'll take no more than ten minutes to go through, and when you're done, you'll be given a score between 1 and 100 that will highlight how close you are to becoming a true long-haul leader.

I will also send you a personalized report based on your answers that will highlight the next steps you need to take in order to start setting smarter goals, focusing on the right priorities, and living a long-haul life.

Visit **longhaulleader.com/assessment** to take the assessment for free today.

Acknowledgments

First of all, I want to thank my beautiful wife and partner in life (and business!), Ercille. Your unwavering support and understanding is something I remain in awe of. I'm forever grateful for that first coffee we shared all those years ago.

To my children: CJ, Chloe (who's also our COO!), Charlie, and Cassandra. Every day, you continue to inspire me. You'll never truly know how much you mean to me, because my love for you all grows each and every day.

I'm incredibly grateful to Jeff Goins and Ariel Curry for helping me develop and edit this book. Your tireless support, suggestions, and knowledge have helped shape every part of this project. Also, to my agent Roger Freet, at Folio Literary Management—you fought hard to get this book out into the world. Saying "I appreciate you" is an understatement. Thank you.

To good friends, old and new, who have shown me what it means to do life right: Kaveh Goodarzey, Kevin Goodman, Pascal Fintoni, Pat Flynn, Greg Hickman, Michael Hyatt, Carrie Wilkerson, Lewis Howes, Jonathan Hopper, Shaa

Wasmund, Jenny Ainsworth, Amy and Vincenzo Landino, Nicole Goode, Ali Abdaal, Mike Morrison, Mike Michalowicz, Ray Edwards, Phil M. Jones, John Lee Dumas, Dale Beaumont, Amy Porterfield, Daniel Priestly, Simon Alexander Ong, Jeff Walker, Rory Vaden, Donald Miller, Jay Papasan, Hal Elrod, Jon Acuff, Ryan Deiss, Sally Hogshead, Todd Herman, Jay Baer, and so, so many more.

I also have to mention the incredible team at 4C Media and its related brands and businesses. Having all of you in my corner makes it much easier to provide value, be accessible, and create fond memories for our clients, event attendees, and subscribers. Thank you.

And finally, I want to pay a special tribute to the memory of my dear friend and mentor, Dan Miller. Without Dan in my corner over many, many years of conversations, breakfasts, lunches, and dinners, not to mention countless Zoom calls and texts, I'm 100 percent sure I wouldn't be the man, father, husband, and entrepreneur I am today. His lessons live on in so many whose lives he touched, and I am glad to have been one of them. He was a true long-haul leader, and I miss him every day.

Bibliography

INTRODUCTION: HUSTLE IS A SEASON, NOT A LIFESTYLE

Collins, Jim, and Morten T. Hansen. *Great by Choice: Uncertainty, Chaos, and Luck: Why Some Thrive Despite Them All.* New York: HarperCollins Publishers, 2011.

Easter, Michael. *Scarcity Brain: Fix Your Craving Mindset and Rewire Your Habits to Thrive with Enough.* New York: Rodale Books, 2023.

CHAPTER 2: YOU GET MORE OF WHAT YOU FOCUS ON

Battelle, John. "The Birth of Google." *WIRED.* August 1, 2005. https://www.wired.com/2005/08/battelle.

Sinek, Simon. "Start with Why—How Great Leaders Inspire Action." TEDx Talks. September 29, 2009. https://www.youtube.com/watch?v=u4ZoJKF_VuA.

"Ten Things We Know to Be True." Google. https://about.google/philosophy.

Yuan, Eric. "A Message from Eric Yuan, CEO of Zoom." Zoom Video Communications. https://www.zoom.com/en/blog/a-message-from-eric-yuan-ceo-of-zoom.

Yuan, Eric. "A Message to Our Users." Zoom Video Communications. https://blog.zoom.us/a-message-to-our-users.

"Zoom Video Communications: Number of Employees 2019–2024 | ZM." MacroTrends. https://www.macrotrends.net/stocks/charts/ZM/zoom-video-communications/number-of-employees.

CHAPTER 3: "WHO" IS WHAT REALLY MATTERS

Brown, Brené. *Rising Strong: The Reckoning. The Rumble. The Revolution.* New York: Random House, 2015.

"Leading Causes of Death." National Center for Health Statistics. n.d. https://www.cdc.gov/nchs/fastats/leading-causes-of-death.htm.

Maslow, A. H. "A Theory of Human Motivation." *Psychological Review* 50, no. 4 (1943): 370–396. https://doi.org/10.1037/h0054346.

Murthy, Vivek. "Work and the Loneliness Epidemic." *Harvard Business Review.* March 4, 2024. https://hbr.org/2017/09/work-and-the-loneliness-epidemic.

Murthy, Vivek H. "Our Epidemic of Loneliness and Isolation: The U.S. Surgeon General's Advisory on the Healing Effects of Social Connection and Community." US Department of Health and Human Services. 2023. https://www.hhs.gov/sites/default/files/surgeon-general-social-connection-advisory.pdf.

Saporito, Thomas J. "It's Time to Acknowledge CEO Loneliness." *Harvard Business Review.* July 23, 2014. https://hbr.org/2012/02/its-time-to-acknowledge-ceo-lo.

Smyth, Sinead. "Accepting Influence: Find Ways to Say 'Yes.'" Gottman Institute. March 5, 2024. https://www.gottman.com/blog/accepting-influence-find-ways-to-say-yes.

Stevenson, Shawn. *Sleep Smarter: 21 Essential Strategies to Sleep Your Way to a Better Body, Better Health, and Bigger Success.* Emmaus, PA: Rodale, 2016.

CHAPTER 4: MASTER EVERY MOMENT

Del Barco, Mandalit. "Simone Biles Highlights the Unique Stresses Athletes Feel at the Tokyo Olympics." *NPR.* July 28, 2021. https://www.npr.org/sections/tokyo-olympics-live-updates/2021/07/28/1021670837/simone-biles-tokyo-olympics-mental-health.

Easterling, E. "Simon Biles Has Her Own Emoji, and It Suits Her Well." *New York Times.* July 22, 2021. https://www.nytimes.com/2021/07/22/sports/olympics/simone-biles-emoji-twitter-goat.html.

Funk, Anna. "Twisties and Yips: Simone Biles Reveals a Powerful Mind-Body Connection." *Inverse*. February 20, 2024. https://www.inverse.com/mind-body/olympic-science-simone-biles-twisties.

Ingle, Sean. "Simone Biles Exits Women's Olympic Team Gymnastics Final over Mental Health Concern." *The Guardian*. July 28, 2021. https://www.theguardian.com/sport/2021/jul/27/simone-biles-withdraws-tokyo-2020-olympics-gymnastics-all-around-final.

Milanesi, Carolina. "The Price We Pay for Back to Back Meetings." *Forbes*. April 22, 2021. https://www.forbes.com/sites/carolinamilanesi/2021/04/21/the-price-we-pay-for-back-to-back-meetings.

"Our Research." Sabbatical Project. September 10, 2022. https://thesabbaticalproject.org/research.

Perlow, Leslie A. "Stop the Meeting Madness." *Harvard Business Review*. June 26, 2017. https://hbr.org/2017/07/stop-the-meeting-madness.

Porter, Michael E. "How CEOs Manage Time." *Harvard Business Review*. July 8, 2021. https://hbr.org/2018/07/how-ceos-manage-time.

Powers, Kirsten. "Let's Make 2024 the Year of Saying No to Productivity Culture." *Changing the Channel with Kirsten Powers*. January 4, 2024. https://kirstenpowers.substack.com/p/lets-make-2024-the-year-of-saying.

Schabram, Kira. "Research: The Transformative Power of Sabbaticals." *Harvard Business Review*. February 23, 2023. https://hbr.org/2023/02/research-the-transformative-power-of-sabbaticals.

"Simone Biles Says Being 'Intentional' Is Key in Her Epic Comeback Toward 2024 Paris Olympics." *NBC News*. September 7, 2023. https://www.nbcnews.com/news/us-news/simone-biles-says-intentional-key-epic-comeback-paris-2024-olympics-rcna103818.

"The Transformative Power of Sabbaticals." *AOM Insights*. December 9, 2022. https://journals.aom.org/doi/10.5465/amd.2021.0100.summary.

CHAPTER 5: UPGRADE YOUR BATTERIES

Charfen, Alex. "900—Final Episodes 1 of 6 What Hustle Should Be."

CHARFEN. March 22, 2024. https://www.charfen.com/podcasts/900-what-hustle-should-be.

"Leading Causes of Death." National Center for Health Statistics. https://www.cdc.gov/nchs/fastats/leading-causes-of-death.htm.

Powers, Kirsten. "Chronic Stress Makes You Sick, and May Even Kill You." *Changing the Channel with Kirsten Powers*. December 6, 2023. https://kirstenpowers.substack.com/p/living-in-survival-mode-causes-chronic.

CHAPTER 6: KNOW WHEN TO PUSH

Dweck, Carol. *Mindset: The New Psychology of Success*. New York: Ballantine, 2006.

Dweck, Carol. "The Power of Yet," TEDx Talk, Norrköping, Sweden, 11 min., 18 sec., https://www.youtube.com/watch?v=J-swZaKN2Ic.

Powers, Kirsten. "Chronic Stress Makes You Sick, and May Even Kill You." *Changing the Channel with Kirsten Powers*. December 6, 2023. https://kirstenpowers.substack.com/p/living-in-survival-mode-causes-chronic.

CHAPTER 7: STAY IN YOUR ZONE OF GENIUS

Ducker, Chris. "Avoiding Overwhelm and Setting Boundaries with Yasmine Cheyenne." Youpreneur.com. July 29, 2023. https://youpreneur.com/avoiding-overwhelm-and-setting-boundaries-with-yasmine-cheyenne.

Hendricks, Gay. *The Big Leap: Conquer Your Hidden Fear and Take Life to the Next Level*. HarperOne, 2010.

CHAPTER 8: MULTIPLY YOUR MONEY

Crosbie, Jack. "Off Grid, Extremely Online." *New York Times*. August 14, 2024. https://www.nytimes.com/2024/08/14/style/off-grid-homesteading-nate-petroski.html.

Jarvis, Chase. "Hustle Culture Never Ends: How to Find Success on Your Own Terms with Jenna Kutcher | Chase Jarvis." YouTube. June 26, 2023. https://www.youtube.com/watch?v=hjd32R6mCJY.

CHAPTER 9: DON'T FORGET TO DO WHAT YOU LOVE

Goh, Amanda. "David Beckham Is a Lego Geek and Says the Toys Help to Calm Him Down." *Business Insider*. October 9, 2023. https://www.businessinsider.com/david-beckham-loves-lego-helps-to-calm-him-down-2023-10.

Robbins, Ron Cynewulf. "The Artist Winston Churchill: Half Passion, Half Philosophy." n.d. America's National Churchill Museum. https://www.nationalchurchillmuseum.org/the-artist-winston-churchill.html.

CHAPTER 10: BUILD A LEGACY

Charfen, Alex. "900—Final Episodes 1 of 6 What Hustle Should Be." *CHARFEN*. March 22, 2024. https://www.charfen.com/podcasts/900-what-hustle-should-be.

"Michael Hyatt & Co. Is Now Full Focus." Full Focus. February 14, 2022. https://fullfocus.co/rebrand.

Index

Index

Index

Index

Index

Index

Index

Chris Ducker is a serial entrepreneur and the founder of Youpreneur.com, a leading personal brand business education company. He is author of *Virtual Freedom* and *Rise of the Youpreneur*. He spends most of his time coaching business leaders and lives with his family in Cambridgeshire, England.

RAISING READERS
Books Build Bright Futures

Thank you for reading this book and for being a reader of books in general. As a author, I am so grateful to share being part of a community of readers with you and I hope you will join me in passing our love of books on to the next generation of readers.

Did you know that reading for enjoyment is the single biggest predictor of child's future happiness and success?

More than family circumstances, parents' educational background, or income reading impacts a child's future academic performance, emotional well-being communication skills, economic security, ambition, and happiness.

Studies show that kids reading for enjoyment in the US is in rapid decline:

- In 2012, 53% of 9-year-olds read almost every day. Just 10 years later, in 2022, the number had fallen to 39%.
- In 2012, 27% of 13-year-olds read for fun daily. By 2023, that number was just 14%.

Together, we can commit to **Raising Readers** and change this trend. How?

- Read to children in your life daily.
- Model reading as a fun activity.
- Reduce screen time.
- Start a family, school, or community book club.
- Visit bookstores and libraries regularly.
- Listen to audiobooks.
- Read the book before you see the movie.
- Encourage your child to read aloud to a pet or stuffed animal.
- Give books as gifts.
- Donate books to families and communities in need.

BOB1217

Books build bright futures, and **Raising Readers** is our shared responsibility.

For more information, visit **JoinRaisingReaders.com**

Sources: National Endowment for the Arts, National Assessment of Educational Progress, WorldBookDay.org, Nielsen BookData's 2023 "Understanding the Children's Book Consumer"